# THE COMPLETE PAINTERS HANDBOOK

## How to Paint Your House Inside and Out – the Right Way

by Gregg E. Sandreuter

Rodale Press, Emmaus, Pa.

*To Mom and Dad, Jeff, and Heidi*

The information presented in this book has been researched and tested, and all efforts have been made to insure accuracy and safety. However, due to the variability of local conditions, construction and painting materials, personal skills, etc., Rodale Press and the author assume no responsibility for any injuries suffered or damages or other losses incurred during or as a result of following these instructions. All instructions should be carefully studied and clearly understood before beginning to paint. Follow all accepted safety procedures during painting.

Book Design: Sandy Freeman

Illustrations: John Carlance and Darlene Schneck

**Library of Congress Cataloging-in-Publication Data**

Sandreuter, Gregg E.
    The complete painters handbook.

    Includes index.
    1. House painting—Handbooks, manuals, etc.
I. Title.
TT320.S25    1988    698'.1    88–4483
ISBN 0-87857-756-4    paperback

2   4   6   8   10   9   7   5   3      paperback

# CONTENTS

# ACKNOWLEDGMENTS

This book is the culmination of the work of many. Thanks to Jon York, Crosby Smith, Tisha Chipman, Shelby Smith, Rich Barton, Joe DiFrancesco, Nic Hodgson, Beth Spinola, Sandra Smith, Richard Sandreuter, Ken Hedley, Tim DiScipio, Heidi Sandreuter, and Jeff Sandreuter for your photography. Thanks to Jim Connelly and Dan Gilbert for your explanations of paints, stains, and methods. Thanks to Betsy Demtrak and Maggie Balitas for your editing and advice. Finally, thanks to Jon Hedley for the impetus.

# INTRODUCTION

When I started painting, I searched high and low for a comprehensive guide to painting but found little detailed, professional-level instruction. I had to learn the ropes alone, all the while thinking how valuable that kind of guide would be.

I've written that guide. This book shows you how to paint or stain a house safely, quickly, and predictably. It leads you through the entire painting process, including how to glaze windows, replace trim boards, repair drywall, operate electric sanders, raise ladders and platforms, and apply a variety of paints and stains, inside or out. Because painting is much more than waving a brush, I cover color selection, paint types, peeling problems, and rollers and spray guns.

No longer will you fall prey to a faceless painting company's estimate: this book shows you everything you need to know to complete the job yourself. If you choose not to paint, this book gives you the background to wisely evaluate a professional painter's estimate.

*The Complete Painters Handbook* promises you 10-hour workdays, lots of humidity and sticky clothes,

## A PAINTER'S CHECKLIST

### Exterior

☐ Remove shutters (watch out for bees and bats). Label and stack shutters, or transport them to a stripping shop if necessary.

☐ Clip bushes and tree limbs back from house. Pick up clippings.

☐ Close storm windows so that sanding dust does not get on sashes.

☐ Remove hardware (light fixtures, plant hangers, thermometers, and so forth).

☐ Begin heavy sanding, staying out of direct sun. Work top to bottom, side to side. Then fine sand these areas.

☐ Scrape. Concentrate on trim-to-siding joints where the sander wheel cannot reach, and also masonry, concrete foundations, and gutters.

☐ Fill holes and cracks with caulk, Water Putty, and Spackle. Repair broken glass and rotten wood.

☐ Brush dust off siding. Wash with TSP and bleach (painted and stained surfaces only).

☐ Remove storm windows and renew glazing compound as necessary.

☐ Prep shutters. (This can be done evenings and on rainy days.)

☐ Prime bare wood. Allow to dry 24 hours.

☐ Paint. If a one-color scheme, paint everything in one sweep—trim, siding, and windows. If a two-color scheme, paint siding first, let dry, then paint all trim. Paint shutters on rainy days.

☐ Re-install storm windows and hardware.

☐ Paint floors, thresholds, and steps.

☐ Walk around house to check for drips, bare spots, and other flaws.

☐ Re-install shutters.

☐ Scrape window panes when paint has dried sufficiently.

paint on your hands, sneakers filled with dust, the faint aroma of paint thinner in your hair, a dynamite tan, a terrific sense of satisfaction and pride, and savings in your pocket.

## Are You the Best Person for the Job?

Before you start hauling out ladders and opening paint buckets, ask yourself these questions to determine if you're the best person for the job:

■ Can you physically handle the surface preparation and repairs that should be done first? Do you *want* to?

■ Do you have the tools and equipment you'll need? If not, do you care to invest in them?

■ Do you have the time to do the job? What would happen if you missed your deadline?

■ Do you feel *very* comfortable undertaking this project—or do you get dizzy from heights or hate getting messy?

■ How much money will you save by doing this yourself? Enough to warrant taking on the job?

■ How committed are you to doing a top-quality job that will last?

These questions can help you decide if *you* should tackle this undertaking or if you should hire someone to do the job. To get a good overview of the painting process and all that it entails, refer to "A Painter's Checklist—Exterior" and "A Painter's Checklist—Interior" before you commit yourself to doing the job on your own.

Most of the repairs and preparation a house will need before painting are easy enough and can be done with basic home tools and modest skills. You may choose to have a carpenter fix any standard problems, so that you can concentrate on painting.

Sanding is an ambitious job, too. I recommend using a heavy-duty rotary disk-sander to do the paint removal, and this tool demands some strength to use and an investment of around $150, should you choose to buy one.

How big is the job? Some houses simply need to be washed before painting. Peeling walls, however, mean heavy sanding. Also consider that any job will take about 25 percent more time if done on a ladder rather than on the ground; the job will be more dangerous, as well.

Estimate the dollar savings of doing the project yourself. The larger, older, and more tree-sheltered the house, the more tools, equipment, materials, and time you're apt to need. Refer to Chapter 1 for help in determining the expense of doing the job yourself. The size of the cash outlay may come as a surprise. You can save money by renting the more expensive equipment, but I do not recommend trusting your safety to rental ladders and planks.

To calculate how much money you can expect to save by doing the job yourself, add your estimated costs for equipment, materials, and labor—giving yourself a wage you consider worth your while. How does the sum compare with estimates from two or three painting contractors?

Assess your own fitness for the project. A couple of rooms are easy to paint and don't require a lot of stamina. But painting an entire house is time-consuming and enervating. You must have both plenty of time to complete the project (everything takes longer than expected, especially the first time around) and the endurance to work hour after hour, in dirty clothes, in high and precarious places, and in variable weather. With all due respect, it may be best to leave physically tiring work, such as using a sander and painting second stories and eaves, to a contractor if you are over the age of 40 or in less-than-excellent condition. House painting is hard work.

Finally, I've seen many painting jobs run far beyond the anticipated completion date. A time miscalculation can ruin the fun of painting and jeopardize the chance to finish the job at all. Again, Chapter 1 will help you calculate how long the preparation work and painting will take.

Despite all of the cautions indicated above, painting a house is still one of the most gratifying

## A PAINTER'S CHECKLIST

### Interior

- ☐ Remove outlet plates, lights, furniture, hardware, carpets, and so forth.
- ☐ Repair split and cracked walls. Make other surface repairs.
- ☐ Hand sand glossy paint on doors, windows, and trim.
- ☐ Wipe away dust and cobwebs. Wash with mild soap where necessary.
- ☐ Lay drop cloths and arrange lamps for maximum lighting.
- ☐ Prime bare wood and repairs.
- ☐ Paint. If a one-color scheme, paint ceiling and walls, top to bottom; then paint woodwork. If a two-color scheme, paint ceiling and let dry. Then paint walls and let dry. Then paint woodwork (windows, doors, cabinets, and so forth).
- ☐ Paint floors and thresholds.
- ☐ Re-install hardware, remove drop cloths and equipment, sweep up, and reposition carpets and furniture.
- ☐ Scrape window panes when paint has dried sufficiently.

experiences a homeowner can have—to do a thorough, neat, beautiful, and durable job and then haul in that last ladder without incident, on time, and at a cash cost thousands of dollars under the lowest professional estimate is a terrific and doable accomplishment. If you are up to the task, I wish you all the best!

# CHAPTER 1

# How Much Time and Money Will It Take?

This chapter shows you how to figure how much time and money you'll need to paint all or part of your home. An estimate is especially important to you as a homeowner, because other responsibilities limit the time you can devote to a painting job of this scale. The figures will suggest whether you should take it on yourself or hire it out.

This chapter guides you through an estimating process that will enable you to accurately gauge how much time will be needed to paint anything and everything in your home, whether it be the whole place or just a few windows.

## Estimating the Exterior

As you walk around the house a few times, note high spots, peeling paint, sagging shutters,

1

and other time-demanding areas. Once you have a general idea of what needs to be done, then get specific. Inventory the things you'll have to paint using Table 1-1, "Time Estimates: Exterior" on pages 4–5. Your home's exterior is merely the sum of many small painting projects: doors, windows, shutters, blocks of siding, trim board sections, fancy woodwork, and so on. By tallying how many of these projects you plan to paint, you get a picture of the magnitude of your painting job.

This table should help you determine the amount of preparation, priming, and painting work for each item. As you fill it out, you'll be using your judgment. All you need to do is figure *if and where* sanding and washing and priming and painting are required, and then look up how long this will take. For more information on just how much attention a particular area needs, see the chapter that covers that particular aspect of prep work or painting.

Keep in mind that the decision to sand to the bare wood means you'll have to prime *and* paint, which is just like painting twice. As you inspect the house, judge how bad off each element is. I've used three categories in Table 1-1. Extensive preparation/prime means that you expect to heavy sand 50 to 100 percent of the surface to the bare wood, then fine sand, scrape, and prime in order to be ready to paint the finish coat. Moderate preparation/prime involves preparing 10 to 50 percent of the surface. And by light preparation/prime, I mean that a surface needs only a little sanding and scraping, and very little or no priming—that is, there'll be no bare wood to cover. Note that I've included priming time in these preparation estimates. This makes sense because the more bare wood you expose by sanding, the more priming you must do. In order to keep things simple, I have not made priming a separate work category.

If you want to know how much of your preparation/prime time will be spent priming, refer to the table. I calculate that fully 30 percent of an extensive preparation job will be spent on priming; on a moderate job, priming will take about 10 percent, and on a light job, virtually 0 percent.

Don't forget to allow for time to take care of ancillary duties. Bushes and limbs should be trimmed back at least 1 foot from the siding, because you're going to need space to move around. You also can pull delicate bushes away from the siding with heavy drop cloths and rope; but remember that bushes still have to be trimmed so that they won't spring back against fresh paint once the cloths are removed. Also consider that you'll have to brush all sanded surfaces to remove sanding dust, and wash and rinse those areas from which you don't have to remove the old paint. (You shouldn't wash *bare* wood walls after brushing—you want to keep bare wood as dry as possible.)

If you'll be painting anything that is higher than two stories (or 20 feet), increase the time estimates in the table by 25 percent to reflect a slower, more cautious rate of working.

When you add up the number of hours a job will take, you may be surprised at how much time is involved. An entire house could take you 6 weeks or more, if you can work only weekday evenings and weekends for a total of 30 hours per week at best. This is a big chunk of time, which is why I strongly recommend that you paint with a partner.

One advantage of working with someone is that the job will be a lot less lonely. And loneliness is a factor in the time estimate for a paint job: when there's no one to joke around with or compare your progress to, you begin to work slower and slower. You won't get clinically depressed, but you won't have much fun either. And if painting your house isn't fun, it isn't worth doing. So get a partner, or better yet, a few partners.

Moreover, when working with others, you'll speed up the preparation and painting tasks: two people painting together can do the job more than twice as fast as a single painter. For example, you need at least two people to set up the plank on ladder jacks. That means the solitary painter must paint from a ladder, which is less efficient.

But where are you going to find partners, especially if you don't have any children you can enslave for a few weeks? The barn-raising strategy is a favorite of mine. You and your spouse get together with a neighborhood couple who also need their house painted. The four of you split the cost of the sanders, plank, ladders, and other equipment. Then you all gang together to paint first one house and then the other. It's faster, more fun, and cheaper, and you may end up better friends, to boot.

After you tally up the numbers, take a walk around the house and consider how many 10-hour days and weekday evenings you can devote to this project. You should allow a comfortable buffer of time, because a few rainy weekends could wash away the hours you set aside to prep and paint. You don't want to find yourself starting in late August and still painting in October: you may inadvertently sacrifice safety and workmanship in trying to beat the clock.

Remember that you don't have to do it all at once; you can paint only the siding and trim now, leaving the window sashes for next year. You also can start sanding as soon as it is warm enough to work outside without gloves, and continue painting well into autumn.

## The More Colors, the More Time

In this book, I use the term "one-color job" to describe a house on which everything is painted with the same color and type of paint. On a "two-color job," siding and trim are painted with different colors and/or different types of paint. And a "multicolor" house involves three colors or types of paint on siding, trim, and shutters.

A multicolor house takes no longer to paint than a two-color house because the shutters are taken off the wall to be painted, no matter what their color. But the time estimate tables take into consideration that a two-color job will take longer than a one-color job. This is an important point to keep in mind when determining the magnitude of the job: a two-color job can take you anywhere from 1½ to 2 times as long (in the painting stage) as a one-color job.

Resist the temptation to reduce the hour estimates listed in the tables. You may think you can beat the times I have given, but there are a number of factors built into the estimates. For example, I know I can paint and scrape a window in 45 minutes, and yet I advise you to allow at least 1 hour. That's a pretty big difference when you're talking 20 windows. But you have to allow time to remove screens and storm windows from their tracks, remove hardware, sweep up or vacuum the paint shavings after painting, and, finally, re-install the storms, screens, and hardware. These tasks are typically overlooked when considering the magnitude of a project, but the little things add up to extra hours. In fact, you'll have to work quickly enough just to meet the estimates in the tables!

## Understanding Exterior Estimates

Now, let's apply everything discussed thus far to a real painting situation to see if you understand how the estimating is done. Imagine that you are going to be painting the front side of the garage shown in Illustration 1-1 on page 6. See if you can put together an hourly estimate that approximates the one outlined below. This exercise should help you pull together all the suggestions in this chapter, which will enable you to see the big picture when estimating your own painting project.

Assume the following: 100 percent of the siding and trim must be stripped to the bare wood and/or scraped until free of loose paint, the garage doors and windows need only moderate prep work, the paint is not thick and alligatoring, and the color scheme is two-color. There are no shutters to paint.

### Windows

In this example, you want to paint the sash inside the storm window housing. The three windows all need to have some glazing compound replaced, but there are no broken panes of glass to replace. So, this qualifies as moderate prep work.

*prep/prime:*
  3 windows $\times$ ½ hours $=$ 1½
*paint:*
  3 windows $\times$ 1 hour $=$ 3
  
  5 hours total
  (approx.)

### Doors

The only doors here are the garage doors. Let's assume that these doors need a moderate amount of heavy sanding and scraping.

*prep/prime:*
  2 garage doors $\times$ 1½ hours $=$ 3
*paint:*
  2 garage doors $\times$ 1½ hours $=$ 3
  
  6 hours total

### "Blocks" of Siding

In this example, the entire garage face needs to be stripped to the wood. You must make a

*(continued on page 6)*

TABLE 1-1

## Time Estimates: Exterior

Fill in number of units (windows, siding sections, 20 feet of trim board, etc.), and multiply by figure given here to arrive at estimate in hours. For example, in the first column, five windows in need of moderate preparation-and-priming work should take you ½ hour each, or 2½ hours total. *Note:* Increase hour figure by 25 percent if unit is more than 20 feet above the ground. For washing or brushing of entire house, add 6 hours (one story) or 14 hours (two stories).

| Preparation/Prime | Double-Hung Window‡‡ | Shutter* | Regular Door‡‡ | 1-Car Garage Door‡‡ |
|---|---|---|---|---|
| **Extensive** (heavy sand 50–100% of surface to bare wood, and fine sand, scrape, and prime; OR large amount of hand sanding, paint removal, scraping, etc.) | __@ 1 =__ | __@ ¾ =__† | __@ 1 =__ | __@ 2½ =__ |
| **Moderate** (heavy sand 10–50% of surface to bare wood, and fine sand, scrape, and prime; OR moderate amount of hand sanding, paint removal, scraping, etc.) | __@ ½ =__ | __@ ½ =__ | __@ ½ =__ | __@ 1½ =__ |
| **Light** (very little or no heavy fine sanding, little scraping, and light hand sanding, brushing, etc.) | __@ ¼ =__ | __@ ¼ =__ | __@ ¼ =__ | __@ ½ =__ |

**Painting/Staining**

| | Double-Hung Window‡‡ | Shutter* | Regular Door‡‡ | 1-Car Garage Door‡‡ |
|---|---|---|---|---|
| 1 coat of paint or stain applied with brush | __@ 1 =__‡ | by brush: __@ ½ =__ | __@ ¾ =__‖ | __@ 1½ =__ |
| | | by sprayer: __@ ¹⁄₂₀ =__§ | | |

*Add 2 hours per 20 shutters for removal and re-installation.
†Or have professionally stripped.
‡Painting time includes scraping paint off window panes and painting surrounding molding.
§Add 1 hour set-up time.
‖Painting time includes surrounding molding. If paint is old and thick, and/or alligatoring, add ½ hour.
#If applying stain, subtract one-quarter of total figure for painting siding (stain can be applied faster than paint).
**For two-color and multicolor jobs only; also includes extra time to cut out window and door moldings with trim paint; if trim same color as siding, no additional time necessary.
††Does not include coating wooden gutter with roofing tar: add ½ hour per 20 feet of gutter.
‡‡If two-color job, calculate painting/staining hours for category: Trim Board, 20-Ft. Length.

| Siding, 8-by-8-Ft. Section | Trim Board, 20-Ft. Length | Fancy Wood-work, 6-In. Width, 6-Ft. Length | Gutter and Downspout, 20-Ft. Length | Concrete Foundation, 20-Ft. Length | 4 Flower Boxes, _or_ 8 Wooden Steps, _or_ 4-Ft. Iron Railing |
|---|---|---|---|---|---|
| __@ 1½ =__ | __@ ¾ =__ | __@ 1 =__ | __@ 1 =__ | __@ ¾ =__ | __@ 1 =__ |
| __@ ¾ =__ | __@ ½ =__ | __@ ½ =__ | __@ ½ =__ | __@ ¼ =__ | __@ ½ =__ |
| __@ ¼ =__ | — | __@ ¼ =__ | — | — | — |

| | | | | | |
|---|---|---|---|---|---|
| __@ ¾ =__# | __@ ¾ =__** | __@ ½ =__ | __@ ¾ =__†† | by roller: __@ ¼ =__ | by brush: __@ ¾ =__ |
| | | | | | by aerosol (railing): __@ ¼ =__ |

judgment call for your siding: if the peeling paint is thick and alligatoring, allocate an extra ½ hour for heavy sanding. But in this example, the paint is fairly thin and comes off like cream under the spinning disk-sander. Therefore, you should allocate the standard 1½ hours for each 8-by-8-foot "block" of siding.

There are definitely two full blocks of siding: one to the left and one to the right of the center window (even though they are only about 6 by 6 feet). To the right of the right window and to the left of the left window, there are small sections of siding not yet accounted for. Even though these corner siding areas are definitely smaller than the standard 8-by-8-foot section, they are tough to heavy sand because they are tight working areas—cramped-in by the main structure of the house and a nearby downspout. Consider these two corner siding areas

as equaling one block of siding. The area of siding below the windows looks as if it equals between two and three blocks of siding. Because we want to make a realisitic estimate, let's round this figure up to three siding blocks. Thus, we have six blocks of siding to heavy sand, prime, and paint.

*prep/prime:*
　6 siding blocks $\times$ 1½ hours　=　9
*paint:*
　6 siding blocks $\times$ ¾ hour　　=　5 (approx.)
　　　　　　　　　　　　　　　　　14 hours total

## Trim Boards

Count the number of 20-foot lengths of trim board. This includes the trim running beneath the gutter and down the right-hand side of the garage

*Illustration 1-1.*

(under the downspout). If you assume the plank scaffolding is 16 feet long, then the following seems accurate:

gutter trim (20 feet) $= 1$
vertical trim board on
right-hand side (20 feet) $= \underline{1}$
2 sections

With the equivalent of two 20-foot sections of trim to paint:

*prep/prime:*
2 sections $\times$ ¾ hour $= 1½$
*paint:*
2 sections $\times$ ¾ hour $= \underline{1½}$
3 hours total

### Foundation

Small sections of the concrete foundation to the lower sides of the garage doors should be painted with a roller. Though it will actually take you only about 20 minutes, allocate one full hour to be conservative.

Also, remember to account for those extra duties like tying back bushes and brushing the siding free of sanding dust. Let's assume the latter takes 2 hours.

### Flower Boxes

There are three flower boxes to be stripped to the bare wood.

*prep/prime:*
3 flower boxes $\times$ ¼ hour $= ¾$
*paint:*
3 flower boxes $\times$ ¼ hour $= \underline{¾}$
2 hours total
(approx.)

Great! You've covered all the bases. It's time to tally the figures, which should equal 33 hours to paint the front of the garage.

Now get yourself a partner. While the entire job still requires 33 hours' worth of work, it can be completed in under 17 hours with two people or in just about 8 hours with four people.

**TABLE 1-2**

| Item to Be Painted | Number of Hours |
|---|---|
| Windows | 5 |
| Doors (garage) | 6 |
| Siding | 14 |
| Trim boards | 3 |
| Foundation | 1 |
| Flower boxes | 2 |
| Brush the siding | 2 |
| Total hours | 33 |

## Estimating the Interior

Go through the same steps for making indoor estimates as you did for outdoor estimates. Your painting will include many of the same items—doors, windows, shutters, moldings, blocks of wall and ceiling area, plus cabinets and shelves. Although it's valuable to understand how long an interior painting assignment will take, it is not critical to your ability to finish the work because even large rooms don't take that much time to paint. You can elect to start painting an interior room without really knowing how long it will take you, and you can run way over your intuitive time schedule without it making much difference: if it takes 12 hours and you thought it should have taken 6 hours, the worst fallout from this underestimation is the irritation it causes. Being able to finish an interior job is not jeopardized by an inaccurate man-hour estimate.

Refer to Table 1-3, "Time Estimates: Interior," on pages 8–9 for preparation and painting times. Keep in mind that interior work requires very careful painting. You need to be much more precise and discriminating than when painting outside, where a small drop of trim paint on the siding may not be noticed.

Interior prep work can take either a little time or a lot, depending on the preparation and repair needed. For instance, it takes very little time if you are just doing a light hand sanding of glossy paint or occasionally scraping loose paint. Repairing a

TABLE 1-3

## Time Estimates: Interior

| Preparation/Prime | Interior Wall and Molding, 20-by-10-Ft. Section | Shelves, Cabinet Doors, 4 to 6 3-Ft. Shelves, *or* 4 to 6 3-Ft. Doors |
|---|---|---|
| Extensive (assumes repair work)* | — | — |
| Moderate | __@ 1 =__ | __@ ½ =__ |
| Light | __@ ½ =__ | __@ ¼ =__ |

| Painting/Staining | | |
|---|---|---|
| | wall and trim same color:<br>____@ ¾ =____<br><br>trim a second color:<br>____@ 1¼ =____ | __@ ¾ =__ |

*Extensive prep work, involving repairs, could take any amount of time, so no attempt has been made to state an estimate.
†If two-color job, calculate painting/staining hours for category: Trim Board, 20-Ft. Length.
‡Painting time includes scraping paint off window panes and painting surrounding molding.
§Painting time includes surrounding molding. If paint is old and thick, and/or alligatoring, add ½ hour.

hole in the wall, however, could take up a few evenings.

## Estimating Materials Cost

Estimating materials is a real guessing game because every job is unique, but this exercise should be useful in giving you a dollar range within which your total materials bill will fall. First you need to estimate the number of hours your painting project will take, as explained above. Then use Table 1-4 "Converting Hours to Dollars," to convert the total number of hours (including time for washing, bush trimming, and so on) to a dollar figure.

This model assumes you will be purchasing high-quality materials, including paint and primer, premium sanding disks, and brand name glazing compound. If you think that the materials bill is high, consider that professionals now charge between $5,000 and $12,000 for a full exterior paint job.

TABLE 1-4

### Converting Hours to Dollars*

| Hours | Multiplier | Dollar Cost |
|---|---|---|
| 0–20 | 10 | 75–200 |
| 20–40 | 8 | 160–320 |
| 40–80 | 6 | 240–540 |
| 80–120 | 5 | 400–600 |
| 120–200 | 4 | 480–800 |
| 200+ | 3½ | 700+ |

*The estimates in this table are general. Overlapping can occur because as you put in more hours, there is more physical work, but the cost of materials will remain approximately the same.

### Estimating the Amount of Paint: Exterior

About 65 percent of your total materials bill will be for paint and primer. Sanding disks make

| Double-Hung Window† | Regular Door† | Fancy Wood-work, 6-In. Width, 6-Ft. Length |
|---|---|---|
| __@ 1 =__ | __@ 1 =__ | __@ 1 =__ |
| __@ ½ =__ | __@ ½ =__ | __@ ½ =__ |
| __@ ¼ =__ | __@ ¼ =__ | __@ ¼ =__ |
| __@ 1 =__‡ | __@ ¾ =__§ | __@ ½ =__ |

up roughly 15 percent, according to my experience, with the remaining 20 percent going to TSP (trisodium phosphate) and bleach, caulk, fillers, masking tape, nails, glazing compound and glazier points, sheets of sandpaper, and so on. Because paint and primer command the lion's share of your total materials bill, plus the fact that you want to avoid overordering a custom-mixed color or running out of paint when the stores are closed, it pays to figure out how many gallons of paint you will need.

There are two ways to estimate the number of gallons of siding paint you will need. Visually divide the house into sections of 20 by 20 feet, or 400 square feet. This is very roughly the area that a gallon of paint will cover. You can simply hold your hands in front of your face to define blocks that are about that size. Figure on using 1 gallon of paint for each block; if you are using stain, count on using 1⅓ gallons per block for the first coat and 1 gallon for the second, because stain soaks into the wood.

■ If your house will be a two-color job—that is, trim and siding will be different colors—plan on buying one gallon of the trim color for every eight gallons of siding paint. So if you need six gallons for the siding, buy a seventh gallon in the trim color to take care of eaves, trim boards, doors, etc.

■ If you are painting shutters, you'll need one gallon of paint for every 28 shutters that will be sprayed, or every 34 shutters that will be painted by hand.

■ If you will be painting window sashes as well as window trim, add one gallon of trim paint for every 40 windows. Buy a full gallon whether you have 28 windows or 36.

To get a more precise estimate of the number of gallons required, you may calculate the surface area of your siding. Illustration 1-2 on page 10 shows a basic house structure. It's simply a drawing of four rectangles and two triangles side-by-side. Once you begin to see your own house as a series of rectangles and triangles, gallon estimates are a cinch. Simply measure the lengths, widths, and heights of each "square" and "rectangle" on your house, and calculate total square feet. For example, the dimensions of the house in the illustration are: length, 80 feet; width, 35 feet; height, 12 feet; and gable height, 8 feet. With these numbers, we can figure out how much surface area must be painted:

Each of the long sides (the front and back of the house) measures 12 by 80 feet. Therefore:

$$12 \text{ feet} \times 80 \text{ feet} = 960 \text{ square feet per side}$$
$$2 \text{ sides} = 1920 \text{ square feet}$$

The two short sides (the near side and far side of the house) each measure 12 by 35 feet. Therefore:

$$12 \text{ feet} \times 35 \text{ feet} = 420 \text{ square feet per side}$$
$$2 \text{ sides} = 840 \text{ square feet}$$

The two gables (one on top of each short side) each measure 8 by 35 feet. Multiply these two dimensions and then multiply this number by ½. Therefore:

$$8 \text{ feet} \times 35 \text{ feet} \times \tfrac{1}{2} = 140 \text{ square feet per gable}$$
$$2 \text{ gables} = 280 \text{ square feet}$$

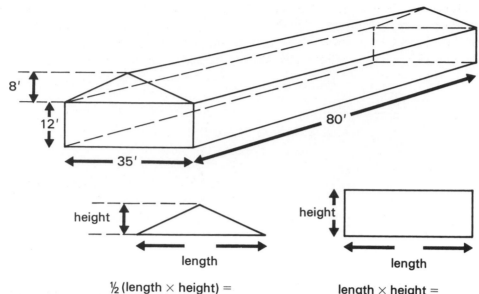

½ (length × height) =
surface area of the triangle

length × height =
surface area of the rectangle

*Illustration 1-2.*

Thus, we have the following measurements:

| | |
|---|---:|
| 2 long sides | 1920 |
| 2 short sides | 840 |
| 2 gables | 280 |
| total square feet | 3040 |

$$\frac{3040 \text{ square feet}}{400 \text{ square feet covered per gallon}} = 7.6 \text{ gallons}$$

What about windows and doors? Clearly, you would need less siding paint if you had lots of windows and doors taking up siding space than if you had siding alone. But the calculation is still accurate. For instance, if Illustration 1-2 had ten windows measuring 3 by 5 feet each, windows would take up 150 square feet of siding space (10 × 3 × 5). Therefore:

| | |
|---|---:|
| total square feet | 3040 |
| window allowance | 150 |
| net square feet | 2890 |

$$\frac{2890 \text{ square feet}}{400 \text{ square feet covered per gallon}} = 7.2 \text{ gallons}$$

The difference between 7.6 gallons and 7.2 gallons is less than ½ gallon, not much at all. When you consider that a rough siding texture can reduce coverage from 400 square feet to 320 square feet per gallon, it makes sense to ignore windows and doors because this automatically compensates for the *extra* paint you'll need if your siding is not perfectly smooth. Besides, you want to have a little paint left over for future needs (touch-up, color matching, etc.). Finally, use the above rules to calculate the remaining gallons required for windows, doors, and trim.

Remember that if you are sanding the siding, you must buy primer and paint. For instance, if you were sanding 100 percent (or 50 percent) of the siding, you would need about 8 gallons (or 4 gallons) of primer as well as 8 gallons of paint, which equals 16 gallons (or 12 gallons) total!

Now that you've figured out how much paint you need, you can determine how much the remaining materials will cost. You can get an estimate by using this rule of thumb: about 35 percent of the total material cost will be for nonpaint items. Assuming a total cost of $24.00 per gallon of paint, here's what we come up with:

$$7.6 \text{ gallons} \times \$24.00 \text{ per gallon} = \$182.40$$
total paint cost

$$\$182.40 \text{ total paint cost} \times \frac{35}{65} = \$98.22$$

So, you'll spend about $182.40 for paint and $98.22 for things like roller sleeves, aluminum foil, glazing compound, sanding disks, and masking tape. Your total will be about $280.00.

If you want to get more precise about where your nonpaint material dollars are going, first make a list of every prepping and painting job ahead of you, noting the materials listed in the Equipment & Materials boxes located in the applicable how-to sections. Then refer to Table 1-5 and add up the costs.

## Estimating Equipment Costs

Once you have determined how much materials will cost, you should figure out how much it

TABLE 1-5

## Price List of Materials

| Material | Price (dollars) | Material | Price (dollars) |
|---|---|---|---|
| Aluminum foil | 1.50 per roll | Paint thinner | 4.00 per gallon |
| Brads | 1.50 per box | Paper towels | 1.00 per roll |
| Caulking | 2.00 per tube | Particle masks | 1.00 for 5 |
| Drywall compound | 5.50 per ½ gallon | Polyurethane | 24.00 per gallon |
| Ear plugs | 3.00 for 12 | Primers | 18.00 per gallon |
| Electrical tape | 1.00 per roll | Razor blades | 5.00 per box of 100 |
| Flat spray paint | 3.00 per aerosol can | Replacement blades for scrapers | 2.00 each |
| Glazier points | 1.00 per box | Replacement glass | 1.00 per square foot |
| Glazing compound | 6.50 per quart | | |
| Gutter track sealer | 12.00 per gallon | Roller sleeves | 3.00 each |
| Hand cleaner | 2.50 per quart | Sanding disks (7 in., aluminum oxide) | 1.50 per disk |
| Household bleach | 1.00 per gallon | | |
| Latex sealer | 14.00 per gallon | Sandpaper sheets | 0.80 each |
| L-shaped mending plates | 2.50 per pair | Spackle | 4.00 per pint |
| | | Stain | 18.00 per gallon |
| Masking tape | 3.50 per roll | Steel wool | 2.00 per carton |
| Mildewcides | 2.50 per container | Throwaway brush | 4.00 each |
| Nails (assorted) | 5.00 for boxes of 4 different types | Trisodium phosphate | 7.50 per 4-pound box |
| | | Water Putty | 6.00 per 4 pounds |
| Paint | 24.00 per gallon | Wood glue | 2.50 per bottle |
| Painting tape | 2.50 per roll | Wood screws | 3.00 per box |
| Paint remover | 7.00 per quart | | |

NOTE: This table contains approximate prices for prepping and painting materials, and it can help you pinpoint how much your painting projects are likely to cost. Prices are those of 1987.

TABLE 1-6

## Price List of Equipment

| Equipment | Price (dollars) | Equipment | Price (dollars) |
|---|---|---|---|
| Branch/limb clippers | 14.00 | Ladder jacks (pair) | 50.00 |
| Broom | 6.00 | Light rope | 4.00 |
| Brushes | | Locking washers for molding scrapers | 1.00 |
| China bristles: | | Miter box and box saw | 30.00 |
| 2-in. beveled brushes | 8.00 | Molding scraper | 10.00 |
| 4-in. siding brushes | 16.00 | Needle-nose pliers | 8.00 |
| 4-in. stain brushes | 15.00 | Outlet adapter | 0.50 |
| Nylon bristles: | | Overalls | 24.00 |
| 2-in. beveled brushes | 6.00 | Paint pot (1 gal.) | 4.00 |
| 4-in. siding brushes | 12.00 | Plastic dish | 1.00 |
| Brush spinner | 14.00 | Plastic tarp (9 by 12 ft.) | 2.00 |
| Bucket (5 gal.) | 6.00 | Plumber's snake | 16.00 |
| Caulking gun | 3.00 | Pothook | 1.50 |
| Circular saw | 40.00 | Putty knife | 6.00 |
| Clamp | 10.00 | Razor blade holder | 1.00 |
| Claw hammer | 18.00 | Reinforced plank | 250.00 |
| Coping saw | 12.00 | Roller handles | 2.50 |
| Countersink | 2.50 | Rotary disk-sander (7 in.) | 140.00 |
| Drop cloth (9 by 12 ft.) | 20.00 | Scraper | 4.00 |
| Dustpan and brush | 4.00 | Screwdrivers | |
| Electric drill and bits | 45.00 | Phillips and flat-head | 4.00 each |
| Extension cord | 20.00 | Shrubbery clippers | 14.00 |
| Extension ladder (commercial grade, 28 ft.) | 180.00 | Straightedge | 6.00 |
| Extension pole | 2.50 | Tape measure | 12.00 |
| Goggles | 3.50 | T-square | 10.00 |
| Hand-held sprayer | 100.00 | Wire cutter | 8.00 |
| Hat | 1.00 or free | Wooden stepladder | 70.00 |
| | | Wood rasp | 8.00 |
| Heavy rubber gloves | 8.00 | Wrecking bar | 14.00 |

NOTE: This table is a comprehensive list of the equipment you will need when painting interior and exterior surfaces, and it can help you to determine how much the total painting job will cost. Prices are those of 1987.

will cost to purchase and/or rent all the equipment you will need. Simply make a list of each piece of equipment you will need, using the Equipment & Material boxes located in the applicable how-to sections, and refer to Table 1-6.

## Hiring a Contractor

If you are daunted by the time and dollar estimates you come up with, you may opt to hire a professional rather than doing the job yourself. If you have a huge painting job, hiring a pro is a wise decision. Nevertheless, your reading won't be in vain. Once you've become familiar with this book, you'll be better able to hire a good painting contractor. For example, you can see if a professional knows the painting business by asking what he or she thinks should be prepped and painted and then comparing this list with your own. (In any case, getting the pro to commit to a specific painting plan makes certain everything you expect to be painted will get painted.)

Consider getting as many as six estimates, and ask for a figure on both labor and materials. Estimates are free (it's an industry standard to charge nothing for compiling an estimate). And for exterior work, you don't have to be home when the professional visits. With six estimates in hand, you'll have a very good idea of the median cost of a paint job. You minimize the chance that you'll get a professional who is expensive beyond the value delivered.

When choosing a pro, remember that reputation is everything. You can locate six painters at random from the yellow pages, but a far better approach is to get recommendations by talking to neighbors and paint shop owners. After all, a large painting job will cost thousands of dollars, and you want to be sure you investigate the character of the individual who will be in and around your home.

Little things mean a lot. Will the pro be courteous and helpful when you have questions or complaints? Will the pro finish the job, or leave the last details incomplete? Consider the aggravation you would experience if the pro didn't show up when you expected. Details make the difference between a mediocre job and a great job, so a more expensive and thorough painter may be a better deal in the long run. The lowest bid is not necessarily the best. You'll want to know more than the bottom line. Here is a checklist of things to put in the contract:

- When can they start?
- When will they finish?
- What type and brand of paint will the pros use?
- Will they spray the paint or brush it?
- What type and extent of surface preparation will be performed?
- Will they sand off loose paint, or merely scrape?
- Would they recommend sandblasting and staining or aluminum siding instead of a new coat of paint, and why?
- Will they wash old painted surfaces before painting?
- When will they arrive in the morning and leave at night?
- Will they work on weekends and over holidays?
- Will the contractor personally be involved in the work, or will a crew be sent in to do the job?
- How long have they painted? Are there homes they've done that you can see? (Ask for a list of references you can call, some of whom had the work done a few years ago so that you can judge the durability of their workmanship).
- Where will they store their equipment? Will there be any equipment or materials that could harm your children or pets?

**Contingency Issues**
- Under what circumstances can you legally void the contract (if, for example, a painter does not start when promised)?
- What if there is damage to your property (a ladder through a car windshield, ruined shrubbery, or spilled paint on the roof, for example)? Who will assume responsibility for the repair and its cost? Does the contract address this issue? If so, is a maximum time alloted for repairs to be completed?
- Is there a guarantee of workmanship (for example, no peeling paint for 2 years)?
- Does the contract explicitly state that you are not responsible for accidents? Does the pro carry liability insurance that covers personal and property damage?
- What if they are unable to finish the job? Are you entitled to a full refund? What arrangements will they make to find another painter to finish the job this season? Do they accept responsibility for extra costs required to find another painter above and beyond the dollar amount you owe them under the contract?

■ What is the payment schedule? An example is 50 percent before work begins and 50 percent upon satisfactory completion of the work.

■ Is the bid in the contract fixed or merely an estimate, subject to revision? (You want to get a fixed and unalterable bid.)

■ Are you responsible for equipment stored on your property?

I do not mean to give you the impression that professional painters are not honorable. But it makes good sense to specify all issues explicitly in an agreement. Anticipate misunderstandings that could erupt into major conflicts. Remember, a contract is not just a legal document—it serves as a way to make clear the responsibilities of both parties, for the sake of a better job.

# CHAPTER 2

# *Preparation*

This chapter takes you through the preparation process, step-by-step. For a complete perspective on the tasks before you, I suggest you read the entire chapter before beginning to prep.

Thorough surface preparation is essential to every paint job. Poor preparation defeats your very purpose—to restore and to protect the object being painted—and virtually guarantees that the paint, no matter how meticulously you apply it, will quickly peel and blister. Think of painting as a building process. You can build more cheaply if you get by with a hastily poured foundation, no insulation, a shoddy roof, and Grade B plumbing and wiring; but over time, it will require more repair and replacement work. That same home, if built solidly, will remain attractive and inexpensive to maintain over the long run. So it is with painting. Because the quality of prep work determines the success of everything you do from that point, pay particular attention to this chapter.

But before you do so much as pick up a paint scraper, make sure you *really* have to paint your house. If the paint itself is solid—not peeling, blistered, or cracked—it simply may be discolored by mildew, dirt, and grime. Wash a small area as a test. Indoors, use a mild soap such as dishwashing detergent and water; outside, use a solution of TSP and bleach (as described later in this chapter). If a bath revives the old colors and restores a fresh appearance, then you can postpone painting. If not, then repainting is the answer.

Prep work includes repairs that should be made before painting. You can use the following checklist to get organized:

**Faulty gutters** allow water and sediment to stream over and discolor siding.

**Loose siding** gives water a chance to damage the home's structure. It should be fixed if the new paint job is to look its best.

**Broken electrical fixtures** should be taken off the walls and repaired. Re-install them after the final coat of paint has dried.

**Crumbling brick and concrete** will continue to deteriorate if left untreated and will cause a new coat of paint to peel quickly. Run your palm over the masonry surface—if the mortar flakes and chips, then the surface needs to be rebuilt or sealed at the least.

**Cracked glass** may indicate warping wood, which in turn suggests that water is leaking over or inside the wall. Check to see if this is indeed the problem. Replacing glass is a messy job, especially if the glass is set in tightly so that the sash has to be dug out. Do this work before painting, so that the debris doesn't mar the newly painted sash.

**Corroded and broken hardware** should be removed while prepping, before it can make rust streaks on the fresh paint. Replace with new hardware after the new coat has dried.

**Cracked plaster and drywall** cannot be mended with paint. The cracks and splits may have been caused by the settling of the foundation and walls or by water seepage, so the problem is apt to be more than cosmetic. Remember that paint is a coating and not a filler, so any but the tiniest frac-

tures will still be visible after painting. The cause of the crack and then the crack itself must be treated before painting.

**Water-damaged walls** usually indicate structural problems. Outdoors, loose siding may be allowing water to seep into the house; also check gutters, storm windows, and weather stripping. Indoors, a broken pipe may be dripping on interior walls and ceilings. Clearly, you should fix any water leak before painting, or the area will stain again.

## Preparing to Prep

The following preparation steps are the result of extensive experimentation and experience; each step is designed to produce the fastest and neatest job possible. And yet the goal goes beyond speed and looks—the materials and the heights involved in painting demand that you consider safety. If followed closely, the techniques in this chapter should help you prep without mishap.

Remember, *preparation is dangerous*. It requires you to operate electrical machinery, handle caustic and toxic substances, breathe fumes and fine dust, and work in high places. Accidents rarely happen to people who pay attention.

Your next goal is to work quickly without ignoring hazards. My experience has been that if I don't consciously push myself to work faster, I slow down. Periodically check your speed and think of ways in which you can quicken your pace. You may even finish ahead of schedule. Not only must you work quickly, you must work systematically. Keep the following points in mind:

**Follow the sun.** When painting and prepping, you want to position your work so that it is never in direct sunlight. This eliminates paint glare and helps you keep cool in hot weather. For example, if your house faces west, work on the front in the morning, break for lunch around noon to allow the sun to pass over the roof, and then work on the back of the house for the remainder of the afternoon. You can tackle the sides whenever the sun allows.

**Have all the materials and equipment on hand.** Before you begin prepping, your garage should be stocked with sanders, sanding disks, goggles, ladders, extension cords, screwdrivers, scrapers, rope, drop cloths, saws, hammers, and so forth. You then won't have your work flow interrupted by running to town to get another box of 16-grit disks and more ear plugs. A little planning will save you tons of time. And keep your equipment and materials organized. Get four or five cardboard shipping boxes from your paint store, and use them to house your materials.

**Carry a molding scraper and putty knife with you at all times.** Then, if you have missed a small spot of peeling paint during heavy sanding, or if dew has loosened once-solid paint, you can take care of the problem without going to fetch a tool.

**Prep with a partner.** You'll do a much better job, and in far less than half the time. Lifting ladders and planks, laying extension cords, and cleaning up go faster when two people pool efforts. The more people you add (up to a point that your equipment and house size can handle), the easier and faster the job. Inside, on the other hand, efficiency goes down if there are more than three people on the job.

**Recruit neighbors.** If you have neighbors who also need their homes painted, try working out a barn-raising arrangement: you and your spouse help them prep and paint their house, and they help you. You then get the advantages of a large crew, split the cost of equipment, and trade ideas on how best to approach painting.

**Lay drop cloths.** They protect surfaces that might be damaged by sanding dust and spills. Outdoors, cover delicate shrubs, flowers, vegetables, brick, and stone walkways. Indoors, cover floors, carpeting, and furniture that is too heavy to move.

**Cover exterior vents.** Covering kitchen fans and air conditioners prevents sanding dust from getting inside. Attach newspaper over the inlet screen with masking tape. Remember to remove the newspaper cover as soon as the work is finished in that area, or the heat of the sun will make the masking tape harder to peel off.

**Keep old towels and rags within reach.** Use them for cleaning hands and tool handles. The local Salvation Army, Goodwill, or thrift shop should have all the old bed sheets and tee shirts you'll need for a few dollars.

**Work systematically.** Work from top to bottom, left to right. If you work in blocks of siding measuring roughly 8 by 8 feet, your attention will be focused on a limited area and there will be less chance of missing a spot. Working systematically is especially important when sanding, scraping, and washing because of the set-up time involved in raising ladders.

**Bring everything you'll need up the ladder and plank with you.** If you are sanding, that means a sander and extension cord. Simple. But you also need both 16- and 60-grit disks, a molding scraper, a paint scraper, and perhaps a hammer to renail loose boards. Painter's overalls have hip loops for hanging extra tools.

**Pay attention to the weather when prepping outdoors.** The night before sanding, tune in the local television or radio station for the latest on tomorrow's weather. Continue to monitor forecasts every few hours while scraping and replacing the glazing compound on windows. An extended rainy spell can wash away the time you set aside for prepping unless you plan properly. To minimize rain delays, you can spend wet days sanding and scraping shutters in the garage.

**Do not prep in threatening weather.** Lightning is attracted to aluminum ladders and electric sanders.

**Be on the lookout for bees, wasps, and hornets.** Stinging insects build hives everywhere—behind shutters, in siding cracks and vents, underground, and in bushes. You must get rid of them in order to work safely, and to get rid of them you must kill them: pour kerosene or paint thinner on ground hives, and use aerosol insect killer with a jet spray nozzle to reach inside small wood splits.

**Be on the lookout for bats.** They sleep behind shutters and under roof trim boards, and the noise and vibrations you make while prepping can scare them out. If you do not *expect* them, they can startle you right off your ladder. Bats may be rabid, so use caution when you suspect their presence. Look for telltale thin, brown, dirtlike streaks on your siding—they're likely to be bat droppings. So, the first thing you should do when climbing a wall with these marks is rap the boards and roof trim with a pole or stick. After a few good swats, any bat behind the wood will let out a mouselike squeak or make a rustling noise. Keep tapping to chase the bat out—you do not want to leave it in there so that it can later fly out and startle you. The bats I've met typically poke their heads out, scream softly for having been awakened, and fly away. Plan on encountering one or two bats in the course of painting your house.

**Wear sneakers when prepping.** They should have good gripping soles for walking on the plank and climbing ladders, and comfortable uppers to allow your feet to breathe on hot days. I don't use heavy work boots because I can't feel the plank and ladder through them, and comfort and grip are more important than support when working this type of job.

**Drink plenty of fluids throughout the workday.** Heat exhaustion can sneak up on you, especially if you are accustomed to working in an office environment. This is important indoors as well.

**If you work by yourself, resist the temptation to slow down and get discouraged.** To keep up the momentum, set daily goals such as stripping the entire front of the house to the bare wood; and then keep sanding until you finish, even if it takes until 9:00 that night. Every hour or so, look back over what you have accomplished and see if you can get just a bit more done in the next hour. The painting process can be deceptive: things tend to take much more time than you expect.

**Watch out for power lines.** I mention this throughout the book because electrocution is a real possibility if you are using an aluminum ladder. Although the power company runs insulated lines to a home, over time the insulation frays, hardens, and may fail to do its job. So don't take the chance of touching wires with a metal ladder. Position ladders so that if they begin to fall, they will miss the lines. You also can use rope to secure a ladder to a tree or the house. Report frayed lines to the power company at once and have them repaired before you paint in that area. Raise and lower ladders only after you look up and check to see that they will not strike the power line on the way. If a ladder gets loose and falls toward a power line, let it go! If it gets snared in the power line, ask the power company to send a crew to take it down for you. Don't take a chance by untangling it yourself.

**If you are an older do-it-yourselfer, you may want to check with your physician before tackling the job of prepping and painting a house.** Although preparation is not as strenuous as running or swimming, it is very hard work. If you are not in excellent shape, a 10-hour day will be tiring and may affect your health. You must be reasonably fit.

## Washing the Walls with Trisodium Phosphate and Bleach

Before any exterior surface *other than bare wood* receives a fresh coat of paint, it should be washed with a solution of trisodium phosphate (TSP), bleach, and warm water. Mix the solution according to the label on the TSP. Exterior surfaces to be washed include siding, trim, doors, windows, shutters, and porch floors and ceilings. Washing with TSP and bleach has two benefits: removing surface debris and killing mildew.

Surface debris (grime, dirt, sanding dust, cobwebs, and chalk) ruins the smoothness of a painting job and prevents paint from adhering to the surface. The result can be premature cracking, blistering, and peeling of the new coat of paint.

Mildew is a dark-colored fungus that thrives on the nutrients in paint and stain, and under the right environmental conditions it will cover entire walls with ugly black spots. It won't cause paint to peel, but it spoils the bright and clean appearance of a new paint job. You have to get rid of mildew

### EQUIPMENT & MATERIALS

#### Washing

- Dustpan brush
- Garden hose (enough to reach the roofline)
- Goggles
- Ladders: extension and step
- Plastic tarps for covering plants and masonry
- 5-gallon plastic mixing bucket (an empty joint compound bucket, for example)
- 1-gallon plastic bucket
- Pothook
- Thick rubber gloves with long cuffs
- Washing mixture: TSP, household bleach, and warm water

before painting because if you paint over it, it continues to grow under the paint and soon will eat its way through to the surface of the fresh coat. Mildew is then *in* the paint and not on it, so that no amount of surface scrubbing will permanently get rid of it. The mildew will always return.

Do not wash bare wood with any liquid, including this TSP mixture. Even though the wood is no longer alive, it will soak up water. This moisture will promote wood rot and increase the chance of peeling.

To prepare sanded, bare wood for painting, simply remove sanding dust with a dry dustpan brush, working from top to bottom. Sanding will take off mold, mildew, dirt, and chalk along with the old paint. Only sanding dust is left behind.

### The Wash Mixture

The wash mixture is simple to make and easy to apply. TSP is a cleansing agent. Just as soap makes your skin "slippery" so that dirt is more easily washed away, TSP helps to wash away foreign particles. TSP comes in powder form and is available at hardware and paint stores. Common household bleach kills the mildew and is caustic and should be used with care. The TSP manufacturers recommend the following mixture proportions:

> 1 cup TSP
> 3 quarts warm water
> 1 quart chlorine bleach

I prefer a more potent mixture:

> 2 cups TSP per gallon
> 50/50 water/bleach mixture

These measurements do not need to be exact, so don't waste time measuring by the teaspoon. Because I mix TSP in a 5-gallon container, I just eyeball for the 50/50 bleach/water ratio.

Here is the step-by-step procedure for using this mixture safely and effectively.

**STEP 1.** Protect delicate plants with plastic tarps. Remember to remove the tarps immediately after using the TSP; shrubs and flowers can quickly die if left covered in hot sun. Plants that have been splashed with the solution should be rinsed with a garden hose.

*Photo 2-1: When washing the surface to be painted with a solution of TSP and bleach, wear gloves to protect your hands. Avoid prolonged contact of the solution with your skin. Wear goggles if there's a chance of getting it in your eyes.*

Also cover stone and brick walls and patios. The caustic property of the solution will readily discolor them. Thoroughly rinse the stone after the tarps are removed. If you encounter some discoloration, use muriatic acid and a stiff plastic-bristled scrub brush to try to blend the discoloration into the natural color. However, once stones are discolored, it's unlikely you'll be able to restore their original appearance, so prevention is the key here. The solution may discolor siding and trim as it drips down, but because you will be repainting, there's no cause for concern.

Protect yourself, too. Wear thick rubber gloves with a long forearm reach. Turn out the glove sleeves so that the cuff prevents the solution from running down your arm. Use goggles, too. They tend to fog up, but the alternative is to get blinding bleach in your eyes.

*Photo 2-2: After washing the walls with TSP, use a garden hose to rinse them, working top to bottom.*

Some people wear long pants and long-sleeved shirts when washing with TSP and bleach, but this is not a good idea: bleach-soaked clothing will rub against the skin, causing a more severe burn than if the solution hits the skin and is promptly rinsed off. I suggest wearing shorts and regularly rinsing your legs and arms with fresh water.

**STEP 2.** Wash with a dustpan brush, dipped into a 1-gallon plastic bucket of TSP solution hanging from a ladder or held in your hand. Lift the brush quickly from the bucket so that you lose as little of the solution as possible, and wipe it across the surface. Do not scrub: the solution does the work for you, and one good swipe with the brush should be enough. As soon as the brush runs out of solution, reload. Do not economize on the stuff—use plenty of it. Expect a fair amount to drip to the ground, and check to see that the plastic tarps applied in step 1 are doing their job.

**STEP 3.** Continue spreading the solution for 15 minutes (the approximate time to complete two or three 8-by-8-foot blocks of the wall, the unit used to calculate the size of a job in Chapter 1. This is about equal to the first floor area the painter is hosing down in Photo 2-2).

Rinse the washed area with a garden hose, top to bottom, until the runoff water is clear. A residue of TSP and bleach may keep paint from adhering. Rinse systematically, moving slowly along each board and from top to bottom.

If you wish, you can rinse the house with a water compressor, available at rental shops. It shoots water at high speed out of a tube, something like a fire hose; however, I don't recommend using a compressor, because it will add to the expense of the job without increasing the durability of the new paint.

**STEP 4.** Repeat steps 1 through 3 until all painted and stained surfaces are washed and rinsed.

**STEP 5.** Let the entire surface dry for at least 48 hours in clear weather before painting or staining.

## Sanding, Heavy and Fine

You'll probably be faced with some sanding before the new coat of paint can be applied. Most homeowners tackle peeling paint by scraping and perhaps with an electric drill attached to a 5-inch sanding pad. A far better way to strip damaged paint is with an industrial-duty 7-inch sander. You

*Photo 2-3: The larger machine is a 7-inch disk-sander. The smaller machine is a standard electric drill, which can be fitted with a 5-inch disk for lighter sanding jobs. Also shown are a 5-inch disk and 7-inch disks with grits of 16 and 60.*

can use it to completely strip bubbles, blisters, flakes, and cracks, as well as peeling, alligatoring, and bumpy paint. Sand to the bare wood with coarse, 16-grit sandpaper until no paint remains on the surface (I'll refer to this process as "heavy sanding," to distinguish it from "fine sanding" with 60-grit paper). When you're done with this step, the freshly sanded surface should look like new wood from the lumberyard.

Sanding is a two-stage process; first, the surface is heavy sanded to the bare wood; then, the surface is fine sanded to get rid of the large cuts left by heavy sanding. Going over the same spot twice may sound like busy work, but it's not. The fastest way to remove paint is to rip it off with the coarsest sandpaper you can get. But because this leaves large cuts and tears in wood that would show through a coat of paint, fine sanding is needed to smooth the surface. Even though you are sanding the same spot twice, the job will go much faster than if fine sandpaper only was used.

For the sake of saving time and money on sanding disks, use 16-grit paper for paint removal and 60-grit for feathering and fine sanding.

Do not leave any paint behind to be removed by fine sanding. (Feathering is the exception to this rule; it is dicussed later in this chapter.) The 60-grit disks are not intended for this job and will quickly clog with melted paint.

When in doubt, sand, even if the paint is only slightly cracked and flaking, or otherwise not completely solid. Strip the entire suspect area. With all of the work involved in painting, you want to be

## EQUIPMENT & MATERIALS

### Sanding

Commercial- or industrial-grade 7-inch rotary disk-sander

Ear plugs

Extension cords, exterior grade and 3-pronged (grounded)

Hat or bandanna

Molding scraper with triangular blade

Overalls

Particle masks

Plastic goggles with side protection

Sanding disks: 16-grit and 60-grit

Shirt

sure that the base surface will hold the fresh coat. Don't cut corners. If a 4-foot-long trim board is peeling along a 3-foot section, strip the entire board. The new paint might have a different sheen or texture if applied over both old paint and a newly sanded surface, and this can be a real eyesore in very visible areas—for example, front doors, garage doors, and trim boards.

Restrict yourself to spot sanding only where peeling paint is localized and overall there is no evidence of pending peeling, such as hairline cracks or tiny bits of flaking. Use your judgment.

Sand the surface to bare wood if you can see different layers of paint, even if there is no peeling. Many painters just scrape off loose paint, leaving rough, unfeathered paint edges that show through the new coat. To avoid this rough appearance, you must strip the entire surface.

All disks should have "resin/aluminum oxide" printed on their backs. Ask your paint store or hardware store salesman for their best. Good sanding disks will last longer without losing their bite. You may have to order these disks if local stores don't carry them. Milwaukee Electric Tool Corporation (Brookfield, Wisconsin) and 3M Company (St. Paul, Minnesota) are two manufacturers of sanding disks.

Do not use disks finer than 16-grit for heavy sanding. Your objective is to remove as much paint as quickly as possible with the minimum of effort. Working with 24-grit and 36-grit disks will take longer, so don't buy them as substitutes. And don't use disks finer that 60-grit for fine sanding. The finer the grit, the more susceptible the disk is to clogging from melted paint. An 80-grit disk will clog much faster and yet costs the same.

Lean into the machine when sanding. The sander will do the work only if it makes solid contact. Normally I push my body into the sander until I can distinctly hear the machine slowing and then maintain that forward pressure. Be careful, though, not to lean so much that, if the wheel catches a crack in the wood and spins off to one side, the sander pulls you along the wall, too. This is a balance issue you can understand only by experimenting. At any given time, you should be able to keep your balance *and* keep the sander from spinning out of your hands or into your body.

Keep the sanding wheel at a 4- to 10-degree angle to the surface being sanded. When the wheel becomes flush with the surface being sanded, the wheel spin pulls the disk in two directions, making the wheel skid uncontrollably on the surface and creating more cuts in the wood than normal.

The sander should be running before the wheel touches the surface and should continue running until after the wheel is pulled from the surface. Starting and stopping the sander when the wheel rests on the suface creates large gouges and reduces your control.

Once a disk loses its bite, discard it. Further use will require more and more effort (harder pressing against the surface, for example) and will produce less and less satisfactory results (melting paint and rough fine sanded areas). Burn marks and melting paint are common indications of worn and clogged disks. Don't be lured into a false sense of economy by working with dull disks.

Keep all disks dry and cool. Water and heat make the disks curl up, sometimes so much that they look like rolled deli meats. At this stage, they are ruined.

Sand evenly and smoothly. When you do not take care to leave a flat surface when heavy sanding, you run the risk of leaving large cuts in the wood that make fine sanding more difficult.

## Choosing a Sander

Any sander can be dangerous if used improperly or carelessly. Because of its power and weight, a sander may be difficult to control and exhausting to operate. It can unexpectedly jump out of your hands and requires constant attention to safety. The wheel rips away paint, nails, wires, hardware, and anything else in its path—and surrounds you with a swirling cloud of splinters and dust, which makes the job uncomfortable. And yet, with a little practice and a little more forbearance, you will find sanding the quickest and easiest way to remove old paint.

A number of manufacturers make disk-sanders. If you have a lot of siding to strip and would rather buy a sander than rent one, I recommend that you order it well in advance of the painting job, because it is a specialty item and may not always be in stock.

The machine pictured throughout this book is the 7-inch disk-sander sold by Sears under the Craftsman label. I've found this model to be very durable, especially given some pretty impressive plunges from ladders and rooftops. Should you choose the Sears sander, I suggest ordering two of each of the following parts:

> Switch (controls the electrical flow); serial number 617805–001
> Fiberglass back-up disks (which hold the sanding disk); serial number 622839–000
> Flange nut (pinches the sanding disk on the back-up disk); serial number 617294–001

These parts mean nothing to you now, but the exploded diagram inside the owner's manual clearly shows where these parts fit into the sander's chassis. It's a good idea to keep these parts on hand so that your prep work will not be delayed if you need the part and have to wait a few weeks for the mail shipment to arrive.

Makita is another brand of disk-sander. The company is known for its industrial-grade power tools, but it's beginning to reach for the retail market. Check local hardware stores that sell to professionals, and mail-order companies that advertise tools in such magazines as *Fine Homebuilding*.

The two models applicable for sanding are:

Model 9218SB; 7-inch sander
Model 9207SPB; 7-inch sander/polisher

The 9218SB is much lighter than the 9207SPB, which means a lot after 6 hours of grinding. A complete list of replacement parts and accessories are listed in Makita's product brochure available at all outlets selling Makita products.

Whichever brand of sander you buy, also order a wire brush cup. It's a handy attachment for stripping intricate things such as iron railings.

### Heavy Sanding

Before sanding a wall, break the siding into visual blocks so that you can focus on a limited area. Then, within this area of 8 by 8 feet, concentrate on individual boards or courses of shingles that need to be sanded. The goal here is to identify exactly what needs to be sanded so you can complete all sanding quickly and yet without missing areas that need attention. Use the following procedure for sanding one board or shingle course:

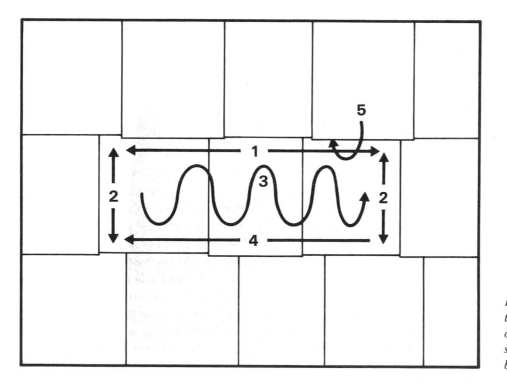

*Illustration 2-1: This shows the heavy sanding sequence for clapboard or shingles. Step 2 should occur at the end of a board or edge of a shingle.*

*Photo 2-4: Concentrate on sanding a small area, measuring about 8 inches high and 2 feet long.*

*Photo 2-5: Heavy sanding along the top of the work area, as in step 1.*

**STEP 1.** With the sander turned on and spinning a 16-grit disk, press the sanding wheel against the siding, and push it up into the lip. Then move the sander left to right in order to remove the paint from under the lip. This stripped area should be about 1 or 2 inches wide, running along line 1 as shown in Illustration 2-1 on page 23.

**STEP 2.** With the sander still pressed into the wood, pull it down the sides of that particular shingle or clapboard (line 2). These sanded strips mark the outer boundary of the board being sanded. The top and sides of the rectangular area are now established.

**STEP 3.** Sand the center, moving the sander up and down in a wavelike pattern, left to right, keeping constant forward pressure on the wheel.

Leave a 1- or 2-inch-wide strip of painted wood along the bottom of the rectangle.

**STEP 4.** Sand the bottom area along line 4. One left-to-right swipe should do it.

**STEP 5.** Sand the lips—the ½-inch overhang at the bottom of each board or shingle (line 5). Hold the sander so that the wheel's sanding surface is facing up, toward the sky.

**STEP 6.** Repeat steps 1 through 5 for the remaining boards or shingles in the block of siding.

**STEP 7.** Fine sand (as described below).

Lips are the easiest parts to forget when sanding, because you don't really notice them. Unless the lips are torn and shredded by the 16-grit disks, you do not need to fine sand them.

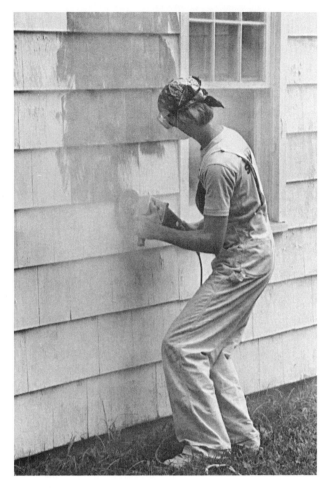

*Photo 2-6: Heavy sanding of the bottom of the work area, as in step 4.*

*Photo 2-7: Heavy sanding of the underside of the lip, with disk facing up.*

*Photo 2-8: These are the tell-tale marks left behind when fine sanding is insufficient. Take care to avoid ripping through wires with the sander. Those that carry dangerous current should be disconnected at the breaker or fuse box.*

Small areas that are too tight for the 7-inch disk may be reached with a 5-inch disk. You can either use a sanding attachment for a regular household electric drill or buy 5-inch disks to fit the sander. Take the fiberglass back-up pad off the sander, secure the 5-inch disk directly on the sander's rubber pad with the flange nut, and sand away.

Be careful to avoid creating flat spots when heavy sanding delicate wooden pieces such as columns. Because the wheel spins so quickly, it can chew away wood in a flash. Hold the wheel very lightly against the surface, and move the sander up and down quickly.

## Fine Sanding

Before you get down from the plank scaffolding or move your ladder, fine sand the work you've just done to avoid the inefficiency of repositioning ladders, plank, and extension cords.

Fine sanding is done as described above for heavy sanding, only use a 60-grit disk. Make long, smooth strokes. A continuous, flowing motion prevents the wheel from gouging the wood and results in a smoother surface.

## Feathering around Corners

Whenever siding meets the trim or the sanding wheel is too large to reach into a small area, you'll have to leave some paint behind. This paint should be feathered into the stripped surface.

Feathering involves smoothing the edge between paint and bare wood. To draw an analogy: you are familiar with sidewalks that slope into the street so that vehicles such as bikes and wheelchairs

*Photo 2-10: If not feathered properly, unsanded areas can be painfully visible.*

*Photo 2-9: Paint is left behind along the column where the sander could not reach.*

can smoothly get from one surface to the other. Feathering is the same thing: sloping the paint into the wood. Just as we get rid of the curb, we get rid of the paint's rough edge by fine sanding. The most common spots for feathering are corners where siding meets columns, doors, and window trim, as shown in Photo 2-9. The goal is to smooth the siding until it feels and appears flat throughout the corner. If done improperly, the sander's circular cuts will show through the paint. These areas not only look bad but are prone to peeling.

When heavy sanding, be careful not to push the sanding wheel all the way into these corners. Instead, keep the wheel an inch or two from bumping against the top and side of a corner. Then, when fine sanding, you have enough space to use a smooth, gentle stroke with a 60-grit disk to create a very smooth transition from paint to bare wood. The feathered area will look beautiful when painted.

After feathering, the corners must be scraped to remove any loose or peeling paint that you weren't able to reach with the sander. Use a molding scraper, being sure to remove all loose caulk and weather stripping at the same time.

Some professionals use both chemical solvents and elbow grease to strip *all* of the paint from corners. My experience has been that the result does not justify the effort, unless the paint is so alligatored that it must be removed. Even when the corner paint is very rough after scraping, you can smooth the rough paint edges with caulk or Water Putty. This will not compromise durability or longevity.

## Sanding Safety

You'll need the following protection:

Ear plugs
Goggles
Hat or bandanna
Overalls
Particle mask
Shirt

Never operate sanders without all the safety equipment noted above. The sander spits up paint chips, wood dust, and nail heads in unpredictable directions; the dust is choking and sticks to everything, especially perspiring skin; and the noise is harsh, constant, and truly deafening. Sanding is strenuous enough; the safety equipment increases your comfort as much as it does your well-being.

Ear plugs are sold at pharmacies. I use Flent's Ear Stopples. These small pink plugs of wax and cotton block out a good deal of unpleasant noise. Soften a piece by squeezing it in your fingers, break it in two pieces, and roll each half in your palm into a 1-inch-long cylinder. Place one half in each ear canal. Stopples should be discarded at the end of every day, because they get caked with dust.

The more of your body that's covered, the better. The sanding wheel can rip through skin so quickly the nerves are oblivious to the damage. At other times, it hurts like crazy. Either way, the injury can be serious. For this reason, overalls are highly

*Photo 2-11: Use a molding scraper to remove paint that the sander can't remove.*

*Photo 2-12: Knot extension cords to keep them from separating. When you're up on a ladder, cords tend to come apart, forcing you to climb back down to regain power.*

*Photo 2-13: Goggles, particle mask, hair covering, and ear plugs are essential when using a sander.*

valuable. The wheel will have to cut through the pant leg before it gets to your own. This gives you the extra split-second to pull the sander away before it burrows into your skin.

Do not plug the sander into a wall socket when the trigger is on. If you have a loose hold on the sander, the sudden kick of power could turn the sanding wheel into your leg. And if you are not holding on to the sander, the force of the wheel could flip the machine wheel-side down, sending it flying. I once was walking by a house when someone inside plugged in a sander. It sailed right through a screen door, just in front of my nose, and landed 50 feet out into the yard. Even if the switch is off, there is a chance that it may have shorted out, so it's best to hold on to the sander tightly each time you plug it in.

Keep your fingers, hands, and face away from the wheel. Hands invariably get nicked, despite your best efforts. Faces, however, do not hide scars as well as hands, so take extra care to hold the tool where it can't jump back at you.

It's very easy to daydream when sanding—to mentally escape your physical discomfort and imagine yourself at the beach, on the ski slopes, or at a weekend party. That's because sanding is boring. And I will admit that a good daydream is one way to make it to quitting time. The trouble is that daydreaming takes up too much of your mind's attention, which increases the chance of accidents. A better way to deal with boredom is to sing, because it keeps you more alert—and no one will be able to hear you.

Do not use the sander (or any other electrical machinery) in the rain. Pools of water and mists can cause electrical shorts in the sander or the extension cord. You should also avoid using the sander around volatile liquids such as paint thinner, gasoline, turpentine, paint removers, and other solvents. Their fumes can be ignited by the sparks inside the sander.

I suggest that you *never use blow torches or heating elements to remove paint.* Even the most competent professionals have burned down houses when stripping paint in this way. Blow torches quickly generate tremendous heat, which can build up behind siding and ignite interior materials hours after quitting time. The heating guns sold in hardware

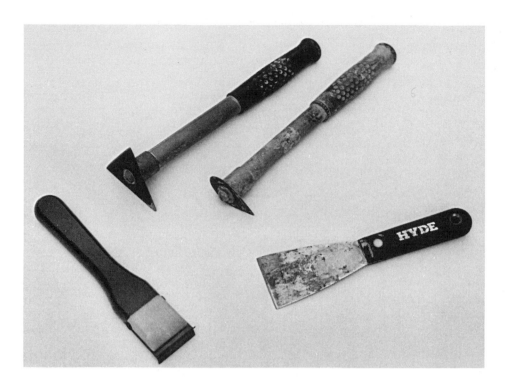

*Photo 2-14: Putty knife (lower right); paint scraper (lower left); and two molding scrapers, one with a triangular blade and one with a teardrop blade.*

stores are no exception, and can heat up enough to cause sawdust and paper to burn.

### Putty Knives and Scrapers

Whenever you can, sand with an electric tool instead of scraping by hand. This makes preparation as easy as possible. If you use the sander to its fullest, then you should be able to strip some 99 percent of the house with it. The only remaining paint will be in corners and other tight areas, where the sander cannot fit or a power tool would damage delicate carvings in the wood. If these small areas are scraped thoroughly, peeling won't be a problem.

You should use three tools when scraping: a putty knife, a paint scraper, and a molding scraper. The putty knife's main purpose is to smooth caulk, Spackle, and other fillers into cracks and holes; but a stiff-bladed putty knife also makes a very good scraping tool. Push the knife into and under old paint, prying it from the surface. A putty knife can slip under old paint that molding and paint scrapers have trouble loosening up.

The paint scraper is pulled across paint to rip

it up from the surface. It can fit into tight areas and allows you to use your strength to remove the most stubborn paint.

The most useful tool in your scraping arsenal is the molding scraper. It enables you to transfer quite a bit of power from your arm to the blade. The blade is pulled across the paint to rake it up, and the point can be dug into paint cracks to open them up for filling and smoothing. The triangular blade is best for scraping flat surfaces and for removing old glazing compound. The teardrop-

E Q U I P M E N T **&** M A T E R I A L S

### Scraping

Goggles

Molding scrapers with teardrop and triangular blades

Paint scrapers of various sizes with replacement blades

Putty knife with stiff, 1½-inch-wide blade

*Photo 2-15: Use a molding scraper to remove old glazing compound.*

*Photo 2-16: A molding scraper is especially useful for digging out old caulk.*

shaped blade comes in handy when scraping paint out of curved and routered wooden pieces.

To scrape thoroughly and systematically, focus on manageable areas as when sanding. Try to remove all of the paint. Often a light scraping will leave loose flakes behind, so use considerable force. Still, there's no need to exhaust yourself; simply be sure that any paint left on the surface after sanding is given the scraping once-over.

For best results, scrape NSEW—that is, north, south, east, west. Old paint that seems solid when scraped left to right may flake off when attacked right to left or top to bottom. By scraping from all angles, you are certain to catch all loose paint.

If any remaining paint has very rough or high edges, feather them. Try a 5-inch disk on an electric drill in tight spots. Or, you can hand sand with 50- or 80-grit sandpaper, folded either into quarters or across a wood block. If hand sanding proves too tiring, smooth the area with caulk or Water Putty.

Don't dip deeply into the wood with scrapers, or the gouges may show through the paint job. Repair scraper marks by hand sanding or, much faster, by filling with caulk or Water Putty.

Keep spare blades on hand for the scrapers. A dull blade makes scraping much harder. One handy way to extend the life of a scraping blade is to sharpen it on the disk sander. First, put on goggles. Put an old 60-grit disk on the sander, then rest it on the ground so that the wheel faces up. Hone the blade on the spinning disk as if it were a grindstone.

The screw that pinches the blade to the molding scraper handle frequently loosens up because of the pressure applied when scraping. To keep the blade firmly attached to the handle, use a locking washer. It looks like a tiny fan blade, and your hardware store will show you what type and size to use.

Finally, use goggles when scraping. Even hand tools can throw paint and wood fragments into eyes.

*Photos 2-17, 2-18, and 2-19: From top to bottom, applying paint remover, scraping off the sludge, and wiping the surface clean with a paper towel.*

## Paint Remover

Delicate and intricate wooden pieces are difficult to prep. Often they cannot be scraped or power sanded without damaging the wood, and hand sanding them usually takes a lot of time while yielding only marginal results. Paint remover is probably your best alternative.

Various types are available from hardware stores and paint stores. Most are methanol-based compounds that chemically interact with dried paint to break down its adhesive bond. The remover causes the paint to bubble and soften so that it can be raked off the surface with a putty knife or scraper. Removers can be used on painted woods, metals, and masonry without damaging them, but they may mar leathers and plastics. Removers strip paints, lacquers, varnishes, shellacs, and polyurethanes (check the manufacturer's instructions), but should not be used to get rid of grease and dirt.

Paint removers are volatile and flammable. Do not use them on hot surfaces or with heat guns. Do not smoke when around these chemicals. Wear thick rubber gloves and goggles, and have paper towels on hand to quickly clean off spatters. Skin contact can cause chemical burns and scars. This is one product you must be especially careful not to splash into your eyes. TSP and bleach will sting, but paint remover can cause permanent damage.

Before using paint remover, wipe off dirt and dust from the old paint you are going to strip. It also helps to scrape loose, peeling, and flaking paint so that there will be less work for the remover to do.

## EQUIPMENT & MATERIALS

### Paint Removal

| | |
|---|---|
| Heavy rubber gloves | Screwdriver |
| Paint remover | Sponge, bucket, and water |
| Paint scraper | |
| Paper towels | Throwaway brush with acrylic bristles |
| Putty knife | |
| Sandpaper | |

Apply the paint remover with a cheap acrylic-bristled brush, and discard the brush after using it. Apply a generous amount—as much as the surface will hold. Spread it in one direction to make sure that it completely covers the old paint, and wait for 3 to 10 minutes without touching the surface. Test the surface by scraping the bubbled sludge with a putty knife, scraper, flat-head screwdriver, or any other tool that fits well into the particular pattern.

If the sludge floats off the surface as you scrape, then you are right on target. Keep scraping to remove as much sludge as possible until there's no moist residue left behind.

If the sludge becomes very soft but you still can't expose the wood when you scrape, let the remover sit for another 2 to 5 minutes. If the sludge has started to solidify, on the other hand, you have waited too long to begin scraping; scrape off as much of the hardened sludge as you can, then apply more remover and again wait 3 to 10 minutes.

If the first application and scraping do not completely strip the wood (and it probably will not), try again. Two or three applications should remove the old paint completely.

Once the remover has done its work, wipe the surface clean with a paper towel, then rinse it with water. (The removers I have used are water-washable, but check the label of your brand for cleanup directions.) Remover left on the surface may later eat through the new coat of paint. Be certain that the newly stripped surface is absolutely dry before painting. You may have to wait more than 48 hours.

You'll probably want to hand sand the dried area, because the remover's action and subsequent scraping leave bumps and abrasions on the surface, especially on wood. Before sanding, *let the surface dry completely;* wood softens when exposed to remover, and the sandpaper grit will rip wood fibers.

Do not rush the process. Let the remover do the work. If the paint does not melt into the remover, slice off what you can without exerting yourself too much, and reapply fresh remover.

Brush the remover only as much as is needed to get it on the surface. Continuous brushing will prevent the remover from settling into the old paint. Also, the more you brush, the more you expose the remover to air, which increases its evaporation and decreases its effectiveness.

Work in small areas. Spreading remover on large areas puts you in a race with the clock. There is a relatively short time interval between when the remover is ready to be scraped and when the remover begins to harden (5 to 10 minutes). You want to avoid being pressured to finish scraping one area in an effort to get to another area before the sludge hardens.

## Replacing Broken Glass

It's best to replace glass before painting so that you don't mess up the fresh-looking paint while doing this work. The job is done from the outside, so you may need a ladder.

First, put on heavy gloves, a long-sleeved shirt, and goggles. Second, remove as much glazing compound as possible from the sash without breaking the glass further. This means you'll probably have to rip out good glazing compound, which will take more time because good glazing compound clings fairly well to the sash. Dig out the glazing compound with a molding scraper and a putty knife.

If you are able to remove all of the old glazing compound, you may be able to lift the entire pane

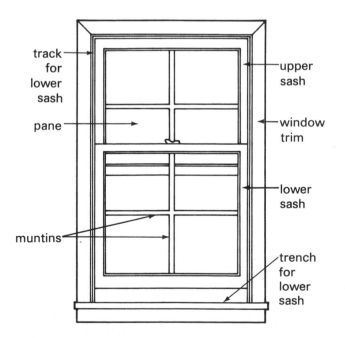

track for lower sash

pane

muntins

upper sash

window trim

lower sash

trench for lower sash

*Illustration 2-2: Parts of a window.*

E Q U I P M E N T **&** M A T E R I A L S

### Glazing

| | |
|---|---|
| Glazing compound | Needle-nose pliers |
| Glazier points | Putty knife |
| Goggles | Replacement glass |
| Heavy gloves | Tape measure |
| Molding scraper | |

of glass out of the sash. Slip a putty knife blade between the glass and the sash or muntin below, and gently push down on the handle to lift the pane until it bumps against the sash or muntin above. Then slowly pull the putty knife out—the glass should come out with it. Once the bottom edge is far enough away from the sash, grasp it and pull the pane out.

If you cannot remove a stubborn pane, break the glass by rapping it with a molding scraper. Have someone hold a folded newspaper on the indoor side of the pane to catch any inward-flying fragments. Your helper should wear goggles and gloves, too. Hit a corner of the pane rather than the middle, and start off with small raps before gradually resorting to more force. After the glass breaks, pinch the remaining shards between your fingers and wiggle them loose.

After all glass is removed, carefully scrape glazing compound and glazier points from the sash with a molding scraper or putty knife so that the new piece of glass will fit easily. Remove dirt and dust with an old 4-inch paintbrush.

With a tape measure carefully measure the aperture or measure the length and width of the removed pane to get the exact dimensions needed for the new glass. I take the measurement twice to make sure I am correct, then immediately write it down. Err slightly on the short side when ordering glass to make sure it will fit. You can cut your own glass, but it's easier to take the measurements to a hardware store and have them cut and wrap the pane for you.

Slide the new pane of glass into place, top

edge first, using the putty knife under the bottom as you would a shoehorn. Do not force the glass into the sash. If it doesn't quite fit, shave off strips of wood with a sharp molding scraper where the glass seems to be bumping. But if the pane is clearly too big, either make another trip to the hardware store or cut the pane down to size—this involves scoring a straight line along one edge with a glass cutter and snapping the glass along that line.

Once the glass is in place, press in glazier points with needle-nose pliers or a putty knife. (Glazier points are small diamond-shaped steel slivers that keep the pane in place; glazing compound merely provides an air seal.) Points must be flush against the glass, and set about halfway into the sash or muntin. Space them every 4 inches or so. Finally, glaze the window.

## Shutters

The storm window has long replaced the shutter as a guard against the elements. Only older and more expensive homes still have shutters that are actually capable of swinging. Nonetheless, shutters are an inheritance, reminiscent of a time when homes had more character and uniqueness. Modern plastic shutters are no more than sturdy plastic sheets molded into wood-grained louvers. They are screwed directly into the siding. New wooden shutters are more expensive and are either hinged or attached directly to the siding with nails or screws. New wooden shutters are more attractive, but they require priming and painting, or two coats of stain, before installation. And in time they will split and peel.

To prepare a shutter for painting, you'll have to remove it. If the shutter is hinged, carefully lift it straight up to avoid bending the hinge pin. If the shutter is nailed, gently pry it from the wall with a pry bar or crowbar. Put wooden blocks between the bar and the shutter to keep from crushing the wood.

Place the shutter on the ground and remove all screws. Hammer out nails backwards until the heads pop out, then pull the nails out with a claw hammer. Use new screws and nails to re-install the shutter, but keep a few of the old ones for samples when picking out new screws and nails at the hardware store.

Don't neglect labeling the shutters if they are hung on pins. Each shutter has a unique pin and

*Photo 2-20: Heavy sanding the shutter frame.*

hinge placement, and it isn't likely to fit on every pin set. Even if shutters are nailed or screwed to the siding, it's still a good idea to label them, because most homes have windows and shutters of several sizes. As you take the shutters off the wall, turn them painted side down and note their locations on their backsides by either scratching the wood with an electric pencil or writing on tape. Labeling shutters is easy. For example, if you have four second-story windows in the front of your house, the pair of shutters belonging to the farthest left window can be marked FT1 (F = front, T = top, 1 = first window, moving left to right), written on masking tape stuck to the frame. Then the shutters for the window far to the right would bear FT4 and so forth.

## Sanding Shutters

Take a close look at the shutters. If the paint on louvers—the slats in the center of the shutter frame—would have to be heavy sanded to remove thick, alligatoring paint, consider having them professionally stripped in a chemical vat. Because professional chemicals are much harsher than retail paint remover, your shutters will come back nearly paint-free. You are then left with the easy task of priming and painting or applying stain. Look in the yellow pages under "Furniture: Repairing and Refinishing" to locate stripping shops. The cost of stripping is usually determined by the shutter's length. Get a written estimate before authorizing the work. Because the chemical process will remove any location labels made on tape, these notations should be scratched into the wood.

If you won't be stripping the shutters and plan on prepping and sanding them yourself, you can save time and avoid rain delays by doing the job in the basement or garage during the evenings and in bad weather. To work on a shutter, place it on two sawhorses or sturdy garbage cans with their tops off. Heavy sand the frame with a 16-grit disk; because the frame wood is only about 2 inches wide, the sander will eat quickly into the paint, so use a ginger touch.

Fine sand the frame with 60-grit disks, and then move on to the louvers. Be very careful when sanding the louvers, because they are delicate. Do not use 16-grit disks on louvers—a gentle touch with the 60-grit will be enough to remove flaking paint and feather at the same time.

*Photo 2-21: Removing paint in joints between louvers and frame with a molding scraper.*

Next, scrape the shutter's face and sides. Every frame-and-louver joint *must be scraped*. This is a chore, but peeling will strike like lightning unless each joint is completely free from loose paint. Paint accumulates there, resulting in uneven drying problems, and because the louvers can move, they pull and push the corner paint. Keep in mind that the shutter will not be seen up close, so a few ridges in the old paint are acceptable. (The joints of interior shutters, however, should be hand sanded if the unfeathered paint edges threaten to draw attention.) Then, quickly scrape peeling paint off the back of the shutter.

Finally, if most of the shutter has been stripped to the bare wood, brush off all dirt and dust; if the shutter still retains most of its paint, wash it with TSP and bleach (described earlier in this chapter). You're then ready to paint.

## Shutter Repairs

Plastic shutters are rarely repairable and should be replaced if cracked or split. The instructions below deal with wooden shutter repair, which can save you lots of money given that new wooden shutters cost about $60 per pair.

This work tends to make generous use of wood glue. Elmer's Wood Glue is excellent, but any brand name wood glue at your hardware store should do the job. There's something you should be aware of before working with glue—as soon as it gets on a surface, it begins to dry. So imagine the spot you'll find yourself in if the glue has been spread but the pieces don't quite fit together. By the time you figure how to fit the wood together again, the glue is apt to be hardened—making it still tougher to get a good fit. So put the pieces together dry for a trial run, before you apply any glue.

### Rotten Wood

Shutters are most likely to rot in the frame joints, where the four frame boards meet. Dig out all of the rotten patch with a chisel, flat-head screwdriver, or molding scraper. Dig until you get to good wood. Blow out all dust and debris. If the hole is deeper or wider than ¾ inch, tap dry wood chips snugly into the hole with a hammer. Smooth in Water Putty, filling the hole completely. The putty doesn't have to be flush with the wood surface, because the excess will be sanded off. Allow the putty to dry 24 hours, then sand it smooth with an old 60-grit disk on the sander.

If the repair is in a frame joint, screw an L-shaped mending plate into the frame for strength, as shown in Photo 2-22. Be sure to screw into good wood and not into dried Water Putty.

### Missing Louvers

Louvers fall out of shutters for any number of reasons: wood rot, a weak frame, the impact from

*Photo 2-22: A metal mending plate will rescue a weak frame joint.*

falling to the ground, or just plain age. If the entire louver is missing, look under its resident window—it may have fallen.

If you cannot find the missing louver, and you aren't able to scavenge one from a ruined shutter, you can easily make a replacement. Cut a stir stick (the wooden rulerlike paddles used for stirring paint) to fit in the frame grooves, making it ¼ inch longer than the exposed length of the other louvers. You may have to pull the frame apart to make it easier to slip the new louver into its grooves. If the louver will not fit because it is too fat, make the ends slimmer by placing the sander on its back, disk up, and honing the louver's ends on it.

Once you get the louver into the frame, remove it. Spread wood glue on both the frame grooves and on the louver ends. Refit the louver, and smooth out the glue that oozes out of the grooves. Allow the replacement to dry 24 hours.

## Loose Louvers

You can tighten up a loose louver by inserting a tapered wood wedge between the louver and the frame. The wedge should measure about 1 by 2 inches and taper from about ¼ inch thick down to just $^1/_{32}$ inch or so. You can make a great wedge by gluing a couple of stir sticks together, clamping or weighting them down until dry, and then sanding them into a wedge with the disk-sander. A coping saw will do a good job of cutting the wedge portion off the stick.

The trick is to make a wedge that will slip effortlessly into the gap behind the louver and squeeze it securely against the frame. Once the wedge fits, remove it. Pull one end of the louver out of the frame. With your finger, spread wood glue on the louver's end and the wedge's thin end. Push the louver back into the frame groove, followed by the wedge. Tap the wedge with a few light hammer blows until it fits snugly. The glue should ooze out a bit—but don't hammer so hard that all the glue is forced out of the groove! Allow the repair to dry 24 hours.

## Nail and Insect Holes

Explore the hole with a screwdriver to determine the extent of damage. Termites, carpenter ants, and bees eat away much of the interior wood while leaving the surface virtually untouched. Pro-

vided the surrounding wood is solid and does not crumble and flake as you jam the screwdriver inside the holes, fill the holes with Water Putty and smooth off with a putty knife.

If you dig out a lot of damaged wood and leave a good-sized hole, patch it with Water Putty and wood scraps. If the damage is on a corner of the frame, you can use brads and stir sticks to create a mold that will hold the drying Water Putty in place.

In the case of extensive damage, you may have to replace the shutter. Do-it-yourself books rarely define what "extensive" means, because this is a matter of judgment. It boils down to this: if you feel like you can fix it, give it a shot; otherwise, save the louvers for spares in the future, throw out the old frame, and buy a replacement shutter at the lumberyard.

## Loose Frames

Frames loosen up because of wood rot, glue deteriorating at joints, and impacts from falls. A loose frame allows the louvers to wiggle and shift in their grooves. If the wood is split, it can be glued back together. If the wood is rotten, dig out the soft areas until you strike solid wood. Remember that only if the good wood is solid and dry can the shutter be effectively glued back together.

With the shutter resting on a flat surface (such as a sheet of plywood), pull the frame apart just enough for the louvers to slip out of their grooves. You want to expose the louver ends enough to cover them with wood glue but not so much that the louvers fall out of the frame altogether.

Push the frame back together to be sure the pieces fit the way you want. Sand down any louver ends that do not slide easily into their grooves. Pull the frame apart again.

Spread a liberal amount of wood glue in the grooves and on the louver ends. Because the louvers have not been pulled all the way out of the frame, you won't be able to reach the very tips. This is not a problem, because the louver tips will be covered with the glue as you press them into the grooves.

Once the louvers and grooves have been glued up, spread glue into the frame cracks and splits, then push the frame back together, guiding the louvers into their respective grooves. Keep the glued pieces pressing against each other with bar or pipe clamps, available at the hardware store, or simply rest the shutter on its side against a wall in the garage and place cinderblocks along the top. Allow the shutter to dry 24 hours without being moved.

### Sagging Frames

This is predominately a problem with hung shutters, because all the weight of the shutter is supported by the frame board with the hinges. To correct sagging, use the same gluing procedure described above for loose frames. If the joints are thoroughly rotten, replace the shutter. If the rot is limited to the joint itself, or if the wood is just loose in the joints, you can get a few more miles out of the shutter by screwing L-shaped metal mending plates into the back over the bad joints.

### Installing Shutters

If your shutters are not hung, then they are fastened to the siding with either finish nails or wood screws. With finish nails, simply renail the shutters on the siding, countersink the nail head, fill the hole with Spackle, and dab with paint. With wood screws, the job is a bit tougher.

Using a variable speed electric drill, drill pilot holes for the screws on the ground, before you climb a ladder. (If you have tried to drive a wood screw without a pilot hole, you know that it takes

work.) If the shutter is longer than 4 feet, it may require six screws; otherwise, four should suffice. The hole's diameter should be a bit smaller than the screw's shank—the core from which the threads spin—to allow the threads to bite into the wood. So that the head of the screws will be flush with the surface of the shutter, counterbore the pilot holes. That is, widen the holes at the top with a wide counterbore bit, sold at hardware stores. At this point, the wood screws are in the shutter frame and sticking slightly out of the pilot holes.

Then, with someone holding the shutter in place, tap the screw heads with a hammer, which leaves a small dimple mark in the siding. Drill pilot holes through these marks and into the siding. Then reposition the shutter screws in these pilot holes, and drive 3-inch flat-head screws into the wall. To make this easier, you should use a screwdriver bit in your drill.

## Doors

Be sensitive to the fact that both interior and exterior doors are highly visible. A poor prep job that leaves paint edges and cuts in the wood will be painfully obvious.

Exterior doors undergo stresses that may cause them to peel. The temperatures indoors and out are apt to be very different, which contributes to wood expansion and contraction. Motion also places stress on a door. A garage door twists and buckles every time it is opened and closed, which can cause paint to peel rather quickly.

Do not remove doorknobs while prepping. Some people have a knack for taking doorknobs apart and putting them back together, but my experience has been that knobs never go back quite as snugly as they were before I messed with them.

Peeling paint is easy to sand off door frames, but more difficult to remove from the panels held within the frames. For one reason, panels are often so narrow that a 7-inch sander disk cannot fit into them without chewing up the surrounding molding strips. For another, panels are often made out of pressboard, which tends to flake off under the sanding wheel. A 5-inch disk may help. You can liberally use Spackle to smooth out hard-to-feather paint edges. Hand sanding, while tiresome, also works well.

---

## EQUIPMENT & MATERIALS

### Repairing and Installing Shutters

| | |
|---|---|
| Brads | 3-inch flat-head wood screws |
| Chisel | Hammer |
| Clamps (or cinder blocks) | Paint |
| Drill bits, counter-bore bit | Screwdriver |
| Electric drill | Spackle |
| Extension cord | Stir sticks |
| Two extension ladders | Water Putty |
| 3-inch finish nails | Wood glue |
| | At least one step-ladder |

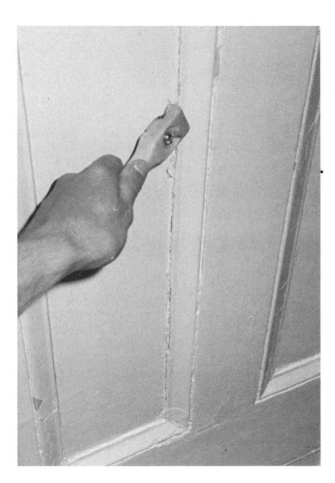

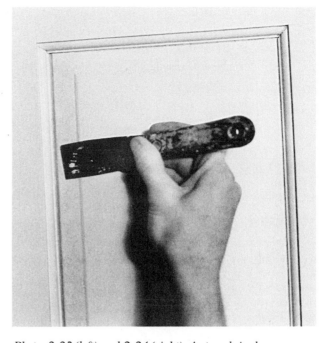

*Photos 2-23 (left) and 2-24 (right): As panels in doors contract, they can expose rough, unpainted edges. Be sure to hand scrape, sand, and paint these edges. In Photo 2-23, a paint scraper is being used; in Photo 2-24, the tool is a putty knife.*

Doors are sanded much like anything else. Heavy sand with 16-grit paper, then with 60-grit. (If a door is peeling badly and requires a total stripping, you can do the work more easily by removing it from its hinges and placing it on sawhorses where the dust won't present a problem.) Next, scrape all corners and panel moldings. Concentrate on loose paint that has split along the panel molding due to the panel's expansion and contraction with humidity.

Feather the scraped areas by hand sanding or by smoothing in Spackle with a putty knife. Use 34-grit sandpaper to wear the paint edge down, then 50- or 80-grit to remove the rough spots.

Now you are ready to hand sand the entire door to roughen the glossy paint so that the new paint can grip the surface. To remove the sheen, use 50- or 80-grit sandpaper folded into quarters, moved with a quick back-and-forth wrist motion. Then brush the dust off the door. If you see signs of mildew, wash the door with TSP and bleach,

using a sponge. Fill all holes, cracks, and splits with Spackle or drywall compound.

Garage doors are prepped as above—except that you shouldn't remove them from their tracks. Just close them fully before heavy sanding and scraping. Make liberal use of caulk.

## E Q U I P M E N T **&** M A T E R I A L S

### Prepping Doors

Electric drill with 5-inch sanding attachment

Molding scraper

Putty knife

Sander and safety equipment

Sanding disks: 16-grit and 60-grit

Sandpaper: 34-grit, 50-grit, and 80-grit

*Photo 2-25: Hand sand all woodwork that has old glossy paint on it prior to painting. This scuffs up the surface so the new paint will adhere.*

Moisture, especially dew, gets under old paint on exterior doors even if it has been feathered well; this can force the paint off the wood and ruin the feathered edge you worked so hard at only the day before. So it's best to wait until just prior to painting to scrape and feather door panels and moldings on exterior doors, to keep moisture from getting under the old paint. Also, by washing first and then scraping, you avoid problems with this source of water.

## Wooden Steps

There isn't much to say about steps if you already have read the earlier sections of this chapter. The only stair parts you need to know are treads, the flat steps you walk on, and risers, the vertical boards between the treads.

The single rule to follow when prepping wooden steps is order: start from the top and work your way down. You'll need to angle the sander's wheel as much as 30 degrees in order to use the edge of the disk to chip away paint from risers. Risers are often too narrow to allow the disk to fit in enough to remove all of the paint. But any remain-

ing paint can be feathered so that risers look and feel smooth.

Scrape the corners well, especially where hand-rail posts meet the treads. These corners harbor paint chips and dust that can prevent the paint from adhering, especially if exposed to direct rain-fall and sunlight. On treads, imperfections in the surface may cause the new paint to lift because of the wear the surface receives.

Screw or nail any loose treads or risers into the stair frame or into adjacent treads or risers. Creaking wood is a sure sign of a loose board. Screws and nails should be countersunk and puttied. Not only will this solve the creaking noise, the step will no longer flex under foot, keeping the new paint coat from tearing away from the board in the future. You also can screw L-shaped mending plates to the underside of the creaking or loose step to provide additional support. Another out-of-sight technique is to hammer wooden wedges, just like those described in the section on shutter repair, into cracks between treads and risers from underneath the steps. This pushes separated boards back together. Molding strips can then be cut to conceal the gaps between the treads and risers on the visible side of the stairs.

## Iron Railings

Iron railings can be handsome ornaments to a walkway or staircase, but they rust like crazy. Metal paint helps lock out rust and covers the iron's naturally lackluster finish with a shiny and smooth coating. If your iron railing is now painted, consider repainting it.

Remove loose paint and rust with a wire brush attachment for a disk-sander or electric drill. Use a wire brush by hand in corners where the power tool cannot reach.

Brush off the railing, and immediately paint the stripped areas with a rust-inhibitive aerosol spray paint. Rust will appear on the railing over-night if you put off painting, possibly requiring you to repeat some prep work.

Spray paint manufacturers recommend using a primer spray paint on bare metal before applying a final spray coat of regular paint. My experience has been that a first coat of regular paint is just as durable.

*Photo 2-26: A wire brush attachment for an electric drill can be a godsend.*

*Photo 2-27: Use long, quick strokes with a new wire brush.*

*Photo 2-28: Use tape to mark areas that shouldn't be painted, and overlap the tape with a drop cloth.*

## Brick, Concrete, Cinderblock, and Stone

Once it starts to peel, painted masonry is the worst surface you will ever prep. If you have large masonry walls with lots of peeling, consult a builder or mason for advice on how best to deal with the situation. Peeling paint is often symptomatic of crumbling brick and mortar, which means going beyond merely repainting to structural repair. Such a job is beyond the scope of this book.

How would you know if your brick is structurally deficient? First, look at the paint chips. If there is more than a dusting of mortar and brick stuck to the paint chips, then the surface itself is contributing to your peeling problem. To check further, scrape into peeling spots on the wall with a putty knife or scraper. If you dig into the brick itself, so that chunks are loosened, then the brick is weak and won't provide a sound surface for a new coat of paint, no matter how well you prep it. If the surface is strong and structurally sound, then you can prep the wall yourself with a high degree of confidence that the new paint will stick.

If the painted wall is mildewed or chalking, wash it with TSP and bleach, allow it to dry at least 24 hours, and then scrape. This seems backwards, but moisture will help to lift the old paint from the surface, making your scraping job easier.

Scrape all of the wall. Work top to bottom, left to right. If you scrape only those areas that are visibly peeling, you will probably miss spots that already have a loose footing and are poised to peel within a short time. Paint is notorious for forming bubbles on brick. These bubbles go undetected unless a scraper passes directly through them and breaks them off. Brush off all dust and mortar chips, and immediately spot paint the wall. Scraped areas that are outdoors become filled with dew overnight, causing paint edges to lift and leave a small air pocket between the remaining paint and the brick. This means re-scraping the same spots. You can avoid this extra work by brushing on an exterior latex house paint (not primer) right after scraping to seal the paint edges.

If the wall is bare brick, to be painted for the first time, wash the wall with a 15 percent solution of muriatic acid. Do not use muriatic acid on painted surfaces.

## Gutters and Downspouts

Aluminum is widely used for gutters and downspouts because of its unique combination of strength, light weight, and durability. Wood was used years ago when the metals were too expensive for residential use, and today, more expensive homes still use wooden gutters because of their understated look.

Aluminum gutters and downspouts usually come coated from the factory with a baked enamel finish. The manufacturers recommend that you don't paint their aluminum, but if you are stuck with a color you dislike, wash them with TSP and bleach, then apply regular house paint, oil or latex. But if you don't mind the current color, then of course there is no need to paint them; you avoid the chance of unsightly peeling in the future and save yourself from unnecessary work now.

Some homes have stainless steel gutters. Because steel is not impervious to rust and discolorations, and it is not attractive if left unpainted, you should paint it. Ordinary house paint, oil or latex, can be used on steel gutters that already have been painted, but use a metal paint on new steel.

Wooden gutters are sturdy and attractive but very vulnerable to rot. To lock out wood rot, gutter sides should be painted and inside tracks should be coated with roofing tar when clean and dry. Smooth the tar with a cheap 3-inch brush to a thickness of about ⅛ inch. One gallon of tar will treat approximately 40 feet of gutter.

If you opt to use a sander on wooden gutters, remember that you'll be high off the ground and working above your head—a challenging job. Also, the sander can mar the gutter's curved underside, so use light strokes to leave a smooth surface.

To prepare a peeling gutter, scrape off all loose paint. Be sure to drag a scraper down the corrugations of downspouts to catch any hidden paint bubbles. A molding scraper with a triangular blade and a wire brush are very effective on the curved underside of gutters. You need to feather the paint edges on wooden gutters only.

No matter what kind of gutters you have, clean leaves and roof debris out of the gutter track. This requires climbing a ladder, so be careful. Be sure the downspout holes are clean; you may need to jam a screwdriver or tree branch down into the

*Photo 2-29: You can use a wire brush to remove old, loose paint from gutters and downspouts.*

elbow joint leading from the gutter to the straight downspout pipe. To check a gutter for leaks and for a pitch that will carry water to the downspout, either wait for a rainstorm or run a hose into the gutter. Making sure gutters and downspouts work properly prevents water stains on your new coat of paint.

## Preparation for Stained Surfaces

The virtue of stain is that it is not paint! Stain does not peel, crack, blister, or alligator, which spares you a lot of the future surface preparation that is a certainty with paint. On top of this advantage, stain is less expensive and easier to apply than paint. Stain's only drawback is that it fades faster than paint and so has to be reapplied more often—perhaps every 3 or 4 years instead of every 5 or 6 years for paint.

Unless painted siding is being stripped to the bare wood, you don't have the option to stain it. That's because stain cannot penetrate the hard coat of dry paint or adhere to it. But stain can be a terrific solution if painted siding and trim have terrible peeling problems: strip all of the paint off the wood, and apply stain to the siding and trim. Your peeling problems have now vanished. You may of course paint the trim and stain the siding. This is a matter of preference. Do you like a glossy sheen to your trim? Then paint that.

As you can gather from this chapter, stripping the siding involves a lot of strenuous work. You may want to give some thought to hiring a professional painting company to do the sweaty sanding or sandblasting, leaving you with the easy task of applying two coats of stain.

If you are sanding the house yourself, strip the surface right down to the bare wood as described earlier in the chapter. And plan on using a solid stain, one with the highest color pigment concentration you can find. That's because solid stain allows you to get by with leaving a small amount of paint on hard-to-reach areas, especially joints along trim, and be confident that the stain will stick. Thus, you can sand the siding until it looks like the house in Photo 2-30, feathering and scraping the corners as normal, and then apply two coats of stain. Note that 99 percent of the siding is stripped to the bare wood, but a little paint remains in the corners. A quality solid stain will stick in these corners despite these small painted spots.

If your siding currently is stained, and you are considering painting it, I say *"Don't!"* Stain is available in all colors of the rainbow, and two coats can keep siding looking fresh for up to 5 years. Paint, on the other hand, commits you to preparation work in the years to come. Eventually, it will peel, and so you or someone else will have to sand the house down. Besides, you can stain a house much faster than you can paint it, so the prospect of applying another coat or two of stain in 5 years does not involve so much work that you should be persuaded to paint instead.

In preparing a stained surface for restaining, take note of what will be painted and what will be stained. Doors, trim, gutters, shutters, and windows are often done with glossy paint in contrast to the rest of the house. You'll need to scrape and sand

*Photo 2-30: If you'll be applying stain to bare wood, there is no need to get all of the paint out of hard-to-sand corners.*

painted items for new paint, then wash the siding for new stain.

If you are going to restain your siding, you must wash the entire house with TSP and bleach to remove mildew. Remember to be thorough. Mildew will eat through new stain almost overnight and, once under the stain, it can be eradicated only by sanding the stain off the surface and recoating. Be certain to wet every square inch of the siding and trim with this solution. Then let the house dry 48 hours.

## Interior Preparation Tips

Interior preparation is just like exterior preparation. Be thorough and methodical, do not cut corners, and prepare a solid, smooth, and debris-free surface for the new coat of paint. Interior prep work must be smoother and more precise than exterior prep work simply because doors, walls, windows, and trims are very close to the eye at all times. But because interior surfaces are not exposed to weather and sun like exterior surfaces, preparation time is usually quite short.

Here is a step-by-step way to prepare interior surfaces for painting.

**STEP 1.** First, remove all hardware: window locks, thermometers, plant hangers, electric outlet plates, light switch plates, curtains and curtain rod hardware, and so forth. Tape screws to the hardware pieces with masking tape to keep from losing them.

**STEP 2.** Scrape loose paint and feather the edges. Window sashes, doors, and trim moldings are prime spots for peeling paint. Also, remember that places in contact with moisture and direct sunlight, such as window sashes, are prime candidates for peeling.

**STEP 3**. You can use a disk-sander indoors, but be aware that it will spit up a lot of dust. Another caution is that the fast rotation of the disk chews quickly through delicate interior woods, so a 5-inch sanding wheel attachment for an electric drill may be a better indoor tool.

Hand sand all glossy and smooth paint surfaces (doors, windows, trim boards, baseboards) with 50- or 80-grit sandpaper. The purpose here is to scuff up the glossy surface so that the new paint can get a good grip. You will leave noticeable scratches in doors and trim when using 50-grit paper, but don't worry: the new paint will cover these up.

To stiffen sandpaper so that it works well in corners, fold a sheet in half and crease it down the middle, tear it in two, and then fold a half into quarters. You can use a sanding block—any small rectangular piece of wood or a commercial model —to take some stress off your fingertips. If you need to reach into tight spots such as moldings and window corners, fold sandpaper around a screwdriver or putty knife and push the paper into the recess.

**STEP 4**. Rip out loose weather stripping and caulks, make all necessary wood repairs, and fill holes and joints with drywall compound or Spackle as necessary. Finish using the compound entirely before applying caulk and new weather stripping; this is because sanding the compound generates tremendous amounts of fine white powder that

*Photo 2-31: Immediately after removing hardware from the walls, tape screws to the hardware.*

sticks to everything, and you don't want that dust embedding itself into nearby soft fillers.

**STEP 5**. Clean the ceiling, walls, and floors. If the surfaces are only grimy, gently wash them with a mild liquid soap and water. Use a damp—not wet— sponge, because too much moisture will soften and warp drywall. Also note that flat paints, unlike glossy paints, are not impervious to water and will allow moisture to soak readily into drywall. If the surfaces are only dusty, dust them off and sweep up. If the surfaces are mildewed, especially in bathrooms and kitches, apply the TSP-and-bleach solution with a sponge.

**STEP 6**. Finally, clear out all preparation materials, let the walls dry, and then paint.

# CHAPTER 3

# Repair before You Paint

Before you paint—both exteriors and interiors —it is necessary to check for any repairs that should be done. This chapter tells how to make numerous repairs, including replacing siding, trim boards, and molding, and repairing cracks, holes, seams, drywall, and windows.

## Exterior Repairs

Even if you take very good care of your home, exterior siding and trim wood will gradually deteriorate. Paint peels and exposes the underlying wood to sun and rain, and water seeps into the siding from interior points. Termite and carpenter ants eat wood. And boards warp, rot, loosen, and splinter. Damaged surfaces such as these must be repaired before painting.

How do you know when wood needs to be replaced instead of repaired? If the damage spreads across the entire width of a board or if the board cannot "hold" a repair, the wooden piece should be entirely removed and new wood installed. Common wood problems are: rotten wood (either wet and soft, as in water rot, or very dry, brittle, and flaking, as in dry rot), split or insect-damaged wood, and small holes and cracks.

Before repairing or replacing wood, determine the *cause* of the board's deterioration and eliminate it. Insect and moisture problems must be taken care of now, or the new wood will also deteriorate. Insects are easily exterminated, but moisture problems may have any of several sources: heavy shrubs and tall grasses shield wood from the drying rays of the sun and keep water from evaporating off the wood, any siding that touches the ground will soak up dew and rain puddles, and leaking gutters drench wood each time it rains.

After determining what needs to be done, plan a repair strategy before you begin repairs. This may sound too obvious, but all too often I have seen people become careless at this stage of preparation. You may want to draw a quick sketch of the project and list, in order, the steps, tools, and methods you plan to use.

## Replacing Wood

Siding and trim boards may be too rotten to be patched up. If they are very far gone, then you would only be masking the problem by digging out bad wood and filling the hole with Plastic Wood or Water Putty. The filler eventually loses its grip on rotten wood and begins to fall out.

To replace a board, start to pry it out by hammering a large screwdriver or chisel underneath and wrenching the tool back and forth. You may need to continue prying with a crowbar. As soon as you remove the piece, hammer the nails out of it as a safety precaution.

If you are sawing your own new board, place the old one on top of the new piece of lumber as a pattern. Align them along their lengths and make them flush at one end. Mark the saw line with a pencil by tracing the old piece. Saw along the pencil line. A good rule is to err on the long side. After all, you can always shorten the new piece. It's like cutting hair—every snip is past the point of no

*Photo 3-1: To remove a trim board, pry it away with a sturdy screwdriver or chisel. You can use a cat's paw or wrecking bar to finish the job.*

return. So place the saw blade on the scrap side of the pencil line.

If you do not feel up to sawing your own new board, or you have many boards to replace, take the nail-free rotten board to a lumberyard and have them do it for you. If the rotten wood has milled edges, fancy carving, or an unusual cut, take it to a wood shop or mill (check the yellow pages under "Carpentry" and "Wood Mills/Shops") to have a new piece professionally made. This leaves you with the simple task of installation.

Put the new board into place, but do not nail it. Given accurate measuring and sawing, the board should fit snugly. If the board is a hair too long, use a wood rasp to remove the spots that prevent it from fitting; if the board is too short, you've screwed up! Boards that are too short leave unsightly gaps when installed. A gap of less than ¼ inch can be filled in with caulk or Water Putty; if the gap is wider, consider cutting a second board.

Once the board fits snugly, remove it and locate the framing members to which it will be nailed. (Note the nail holes in the old piece.) Hammer finish nails into the board, then refit the board and hammer the nails into the framing members. Now countersink them, putty the nail holes, and you're done.

Even if the lumber has been kiln-dried to resist warping, sap can run to the surface within 6 months and discolor paint and stain. So, cover knots by brushing on an oil-based knot sealer before painting. Knot sealer is available at hardware and paint stores.

### Replacing Molding

Molding is the trim that runs around doors, windows, and cabinets; it also runs along the joints between walls and the floor or ceiling. It simply

*Photo 3-2: Lay the piece to be replaced on top of the new wood as a pattern. When sawing, be sure to saw on the scrap side of the pencil line.*

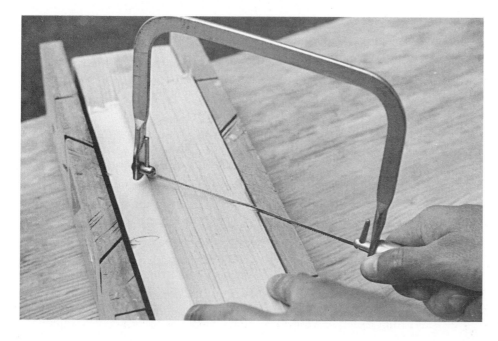

*Photo 3-3: Making a 45-degree cut in a piece of molding with a coping saw and miter box.*

*Photo 3-4: A variety of fillers and sealers are useful for prep work.*

acts as a decorative wood strip that fits between two surfaces to hide rough edges. There is a good chance you will have to replace molding strips. They can be tricky to cut and are an eyesore if sloppily fitted. Nevertheless, properly cut and installed molding not only adorns your work but also can hide any small gaps your predecessor's fledgling woodworking hands left behind.

Molding strips often end at a 45-degree angle, and this is difficult to saw with accuracy. A miter box comes in handy here. It has grooves that hold a saw blade at perfect 30-degree or 45-degree angles. Use either a panel saw or a coping saw with the box. I find that a coping saw's very fine teeth will cut without splintering the wood. For tips on making accurate cuts on molding, consult a book on general carpentry or renovation such as *Carpentry* (Sterling Publishing Co., 1984), by Gaspar J. Lewis.

## Fillers and Sealers

A good hardware store carries countless products used to patch cracks and fill holes indoors and outdoors. To make sure that you will be using fresh fillers and sealers, buy only as much as you'll need in the near future, and seal containers well.

## Caulk

Caulk is a versatile weatherproofing compound for small cracks, seams, ant and bee holes, and splits that might allow water and wind to creep through. It is probably the most durable and easiest to use sealer available. Latex caulk can be worked with the fingers, but silicone caulk should be kept off skin and clothing.

Caulk's greatest advantage is the ability to form an airtight and watertight seal, which makes it ideal for outdoor use around windows, doors, trim boards, air conditioners, and gutters. Caulk also does a great job of smoothing defects in wood and rough areas such as nail holes and molding fractures. It can be used indoors around doors, windows, and trim boards when you want to seal out the elements and get rid of unsightly splits in the woodwork. A disadvantage is that it cannot be sanded, meaning you must apply it smoothly or you'll be stuck with a bumpy surface.

Caulk can be applied to any opening up to ½ inch thick, wide, or deep. Its rubbery consistency allows it to stretch and squish as the wood expands and contracts with changes in moisture and temperature. Because caulking is a simple task and comes at the end of the preparation chores, it can be one of the most satisfying parts of prepara-

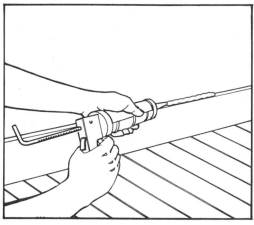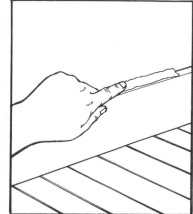

*Illustration 3-1: A caulking bead is applied by either pushing or pulling the caulking gun along the surface. Then smooth the bead of caulk with your finger, if the caulk is latex based, or by pulling a putty knife or plastic spoon along the bead.*

*Photos 3-5 and 3-6: Caulk can cover a multitude of weathering problems. Here, it is used to repair a porch post. Smooth caulk immediately after application.*

*Photo 3-7: On this railing, nail holes and the gap at the post have been filled with caulk.*

*Photo 3-8: Water Putty should be mixed to a consistency like that of oatmeal.*

tion. After sanding, caulking is a piece of cake. And it's sort of a legitimate regression back to finger-painting days.

Caulk comes in a tube that is inserted base first into a metal holder called a caulking gun (the gun forces the caulk through the tube's nozzle). Cut the nozzle at an angle, using a utility knife or razor, then stick a long nail or wire coat hanger into the nozzle to puncture the inner seal. Turn the pressure pin that sticks out the back of the gun so that its teeth engage with the trigger, and pull the trigger.

The caulk will come oozing out the nozzle. To stop the caulk flow, release the pressure pin by turning and pulling it back, just as the caulk starts flowing. With practice, you will develop a feel for the trigger so that you can easily regulate the caulk flow without having to disengage the pin.

Be sure to sweep out and blow away all dirt and dust from the spot to be caulked. Rip out old, dried caulk with a scraper or screwdriver. The area must be dry, or trapped moisture under the caulk can cause paint to split. When you are ready to caulk, place the nozzle on the surface you wish to caulk, gently squeeze the trigger, and either pull or push the gun along the surface—both styles have their followers. To smooth the bead of caulk, you can pull a putty knife or plastic spoon along it or even use your finger if the caulk is latex-based.

Unless you use all of the caulk in a tube, seal the nozzle tightly by plugging it with a nail that is slightly wider than the hole. Otherwise, caulk will harden in the nozzle and the tube will be worthless.

## Water Putty

Durham's Water Putty is the brand name for a yellowish powder that is mixed with water to make an amber paste for filling holes and cracks. This paste dries hard as a rock in as little as 20 minutes for small applications. Water Putty is especially useful for filling an area that is too large for caulk. Although caulk is perfect for fissures less than ½ inch across, Water Putty is best suited for large gaps.

Water Putty is not an epoxy but a powdered plastic. Epoxies are mixed with a hardening cream to cause a heat-generating chemical solidification. Water Putty involves no such chemical reaction and is nontoxic.

Water Putty dries very quickly, so you must be ready to apply it immediately after mixing. It's tricky to mix as well. A tad too little water and the paste will be difficult to smooth out; a hair too much water and the paste becomes so watery that it will stick to nothing.

Your first experience with mixing will involve going back and forth between water and powder to achieve the right consistency. Don't be disappointed if, by the time you're ready to patch the wood, the stuff is already semidry. The key here is practice. As with many of the skills involved in painting, this mixing process is one that you will soon gain a feel

*Photos 3-9, 3-10, 3-11, and 3-12: To help the putty to fill a hole, snugly fit a scrap of wood as shown in the photo above. Press putty into the hole (below), and sand when dry (top right). Be sure the putty has filled the hole completely (bottom right).*

for. Expect your first try to be an unproductive experiment.

To mix Water Putty, pour about 3 cups of the powder into a disposable container, such as a clean margarine tub. Add water slowly and conservatively, mixing it into the powder with your fingers. Add a little powder or water as necessary to get a thick paste. Once the putty is just thick enough so that it slides slowly off your hand, squeeze it to get the lumps out.

Using your fingers, force the putty into cracks, splits, and holes. Apply a good amount of pressure to be sure that you completely fill the crevice. If the crevice is larger than ½ inch across, press a wood scrap into the crevice to give the putty more surface area to grip, as shown in Photo 3-9. Completely cover the hole with putty (Photo 3-10). Let the Water Putty dry. Depending on how thick you have applied it, drying time will range between 1 and 12 hours. A uniform yellow color indicates that the putty is completely dry; a darker center tells you that the putty needs more time.

Smooth the dried putty with a sander; use an old 60-grit disk, because the putty quickly clogs and ruins the paper. Make certain that the putty indeed filled the hole completely. If not, smooth more putty or caulk in the remaining gaps.

If an entire chunk of a trim board or post has rotted away, you can fill the hole with Water Putty by using a simple mold. You'll need brads (small finish nails), stir sticks, and a hammer.

Dig out all the rotten wood from the area to be repaired. Do a thorough job, so that the post has a fighting chance of avoiding further rot. Saw the stir sticks a few inches longer than the area to be molded (see Photo 3-15). Gently tap the brads into the sticks. Press mixed Water Putty into the cavity, and quickly place the sticks against the wood to hold the putty in place. Hammer the brads halfway in so that they can be easily removed later on. Press more putty into the cavity to make sure that there are no air bubbles. Allow the putty to dry completely, then remove the stick molds and sand smooth with a sander and an old 60-grit disk.

This mold technique works well on both flat surfaces and 90-degree corners. It's messy—especially the hammering part—but warm water quickly cleans putty from tools and hands.

*Photos 3-13, 3-14, and 3-15: To patch a large gap such as the one in the base of this porch post, fill the hole with putty (middle photo) and then build a dam of scrap wood (bottom photo).*

## Interior Repairs

The best painting techniques will be lost on drywall or plaster that has holes, cracks, and seams that need repairing. A little attention to these prior to painting is time well spent and will result in a better paint job.

### Drywall Compound

Drywall compound is a water-soluble paste used to fill joints, nail holes, gaps, and other defects in drywall (known also as Sheetrock, gypsum board, plasterboard, and wallboard). These sheets are nailed to wall studs to form interior walls and ceilings. Drywall compound is then spread over nail holes and joints between sheets and later sanded, leaving a smooth surface for painting. Drywall compound is also used for repairs.

Drywall compound is nontoxic. It dries in 24 to 48 hours, depending on thickness of application, and should be primed before painting. Have a building supply center show you its best brand. Before you buy any, check its consistency: it should be creamy white, with no amber, oily surface residue. Whether you are filling a split in the wall, covering a few nail holes, or preparing a new section of drywall, the technique is basically the same: knife the compound on, let it dry, knife more on, let it dry, and sand smooth.

### Cracks and Dents

To repair small cracks and dents, first dig the crack out to remove all loose plaster and dust. This requires digging past the mere loose debris and going into the good drywall. Use a molding scraper

---

## EQUIPMENT **&** MATERIALS

### Drywall

| | |
|---|---|
| Drywall compound | Sandpaper: 36-grit, 50-grit, and 80-grit |
| Drywall knife | |
| Joint tape | Utility knife |
| Molding scraper or screwdriver | |

---

or a screwdriver. If necessary, wash the wall with warm water and a mild liquid soap.

If you are using a putty knife, you can simply scoop compound out of the bucket. But a drywall knife is too wide, so you'll first have to scoop it up from the bucket and lay it on a flat surface—the bottom of a trowel held upside down in your free hand, or a piece of scrap plywood resting near the work site—and then load the drywall knife from this surface. Spread drywall compound well into the crack or dent with a putty knife or, for larger areas, a wide-bladed drywall knife. Smooth the compound out. It should not be more than ¼ inch thick at any point, to ensure proper drying. Chances are that there will still be evidence of a larger crack or dent after a single coat, because the compound shrinks as it dries. After the first coat has dried, apply a second coat. The goal is to spread the compound thick enough that when dry you can't detect the cavity with your fingertips. Excess compound is not a problem, because it will be sanded off later, so don't be too concerned with perfect smoothness at this point.

Let the second coat of compound dry thoroughly. If a third coat isn't necessary, hand sand the area with 50-grit sandpaper so that the compound is smooth, and feather its edges into the wall so well that you can't detect the repair by touch. You can also smooth the compound with an electric pad sander; instead of sandpaper, use a long-lasting screen abrasive made for that purpose.

Sanding creates a very fine white powder that floats over everything in the room. If you are compounding a small crack, you need only cover nearby furniture with plastic tarps. But if you are compounding a larger area, be sure to move all furniture, rugs, and lamps from the room. You may want to seal off open doorways with plastic tarps in order to protect the rest of the house.

### Large Cracks and Splits

If the damage is large or if you are putting up new drywall, you will need to use joint tape to give support to the drying drywall compound. The tape does this by distributing the weight of the compound over a larger area, reducing the likelihood that the dried compound will split along the original crack. After filling the wall's wound, press a

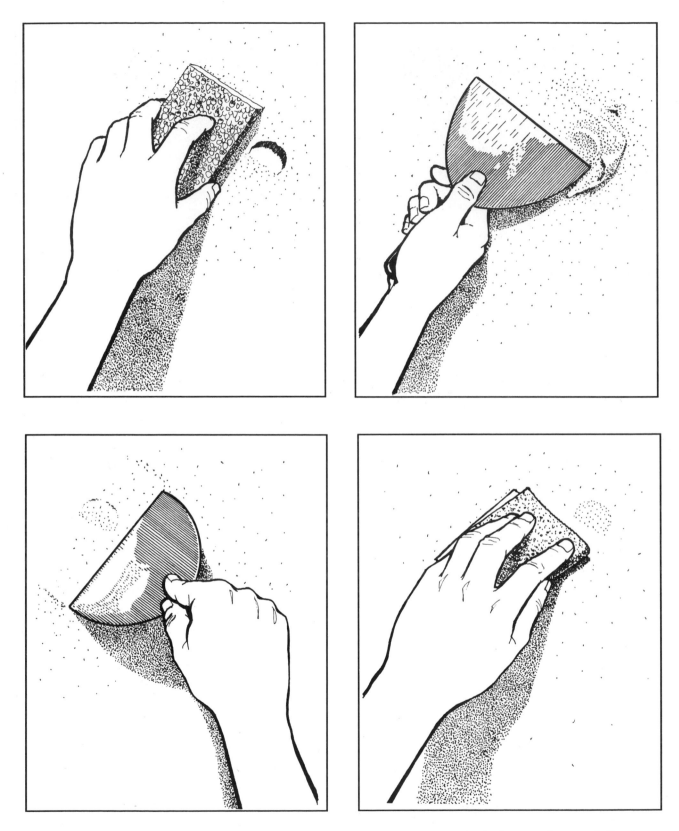

*Illustration 3-2: To repair a small dent, remove loose plaster and dust. Use a drywall knife to spread and smooth the compound into the hole. Apply a second coat and allow it to dry. Sand to smooth and to remove any excess compound.*

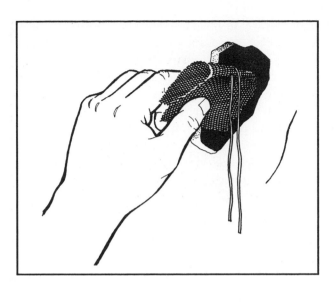

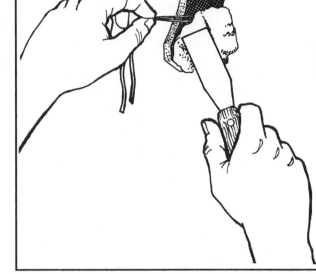

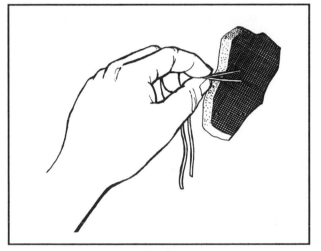

*Illustration 3-3: The first step in repairing a small hole in drywall is to remove all of the loose drywall pieces. Cut a piece of screen at least 1 inch wider than the hole, and thread a knotted piece of string through it. Squeeze the screen through the hole, and pull the screen flat against the inside of the hole. Apply one to three coats of plastering compound, as needed.*

piece of tape into the wet compound, directly over the crack. Make sure that no air bubbles are caught under the tape. Then proceed as described above for smaller problems.

## Holes in Drywall

These directions apply for holes less than 3 inches across. Dig out all loose drywall pieces with a molding scraper and a putty knife. Cut a piece of window screen at least an inch wider than the hole. If the screen is nylon rather than metal, use two or three thicknesses. (Cardboard will also suffice if you don't have any scrap screen.) Place a knot in one end of a piece of string, and thread the string

through the center of the screen. Then squeeze the screen through the hole, and pull the string to flatten the screen against the inside of the hole. While holding the string taut, press a premixed plastering compound (available at hardware stores) into the hole. Drywall compound would take too long to dry for this use, but plastering compound dries in only 30 minutes. Smooth it as described above for cracks and dents, and allow it to dry. Apply second and third coats as needed, keeping the string taut as you press new plaster into the hole. Plastering compound is harder to hand sand than drywall compound, so try to smooth the final coat as best you can. Cut the string flush to the repair before applying the final coat, being sure to cover the loose string end with plaster. Let the final coat dry for 24 hours before sanding lightly.

A hole greater than 3 inches in diameter should be filled with a piece of drywall. Water damage also may necessitate replacing a section of soggy drywall. First cut a patch of drywall with a utility knife, making it an inch or two larger than the hole. Whatever shape you make this piece, use a straight-edge to keep your pencil lines straight. (Note that drywall has a primed side that is intended to show.)

Place this patch over the hole. It should cover the hole completely. With a pencil, trace the perimeter of the patch on the wall. Check to see that the pencil line is between 1 and 2 inches away from the hole at all points.

Following this outline, cut out the damaged area with the utility knife. You need a good deal of force to cut drywall. Make several passes if necessary. *Be sure to angle the utility knife inward,* toward the hole, so that the hole is larger on your side. This keeps the drywall patch from falling through the wall.

Once the beveled hole has been cut out of the wall, sculpt the edge of the patch to fit the hole. Do this by placing it on a table, unfinished side up, and angling the knife 45 degrees. Place the piece into the hole. It should be perfectly flush with the wall. If it is too far in or too far out, the error will show through your soon-to-come coat of paint, a sure sign that an amateur tried to fix the wall. By hand sanding at sticky points, you can get a piece that's too large to fit like a glove. Then, compound the joints as described for cracks and dents.

### Patching Plaster

If your home is over 30 years old, you might encounter plaster-on-lath walls. You can repair small holes and cracks in them with premixed plastering compound or drywall compound from a hardware store. The techniques for plaster repair are the same as described above for drywall. Dig out the crack; knife the plaster into the crevice; let it dry; apply a second coat, if necessary; sand; and paint. Remember that plaster dries faster than drywall compound, so you must move quickly and restrict yourself to smaller areas.

These small spot repairs for plaster walls are easy. But if you have a bigger job, call in a professional. Plastering is a craft, and extensive experience is needed to properly rebuild the wooden lath and apply the plaster smoothly. I once began restoring a plaster foyer and soon found I was over my head. I revised my strategy, ripping down all the plaster and putting up new drywall. If your plaster walls are beyond patching repair, consult a contractor to determine the best solution. Plaster will crack in a house that is settling or shifting, so the damage may indicate larger concerns.

### Spackle and Plastic Wood

Both of these products can be used to fill holes. Spackle is a filler that is applied with a putty knife, much like drywall compound. Use it to fill smaller holes and cracks in wood, plaster, and drywall. Spackle has the advantage of drying quickly—it can be sanded smooth within hours of application. You can apply exterior and interior paints directly over Spackle, without priming.

Plastic Wood is the brand name for a filler made from natural polymers found in plants. It is best suited for filling finish nail holes and other small holes and cracks. Plastic Wood can also be used on metal, glass, and stone, but I find that best results are obtained on wood. Plastic Wood can be sanded, painted, and stained. It not only resembles wood when dry, but it is also water resistant. Plastic Wood contains acetone, a highly volatile and flammable liquid, so do not smoke or use heating elements around it. Plastic Wood is toxic.

## Preparing Windows

Most do-it-yourselfers become disenchanted with preparation work when it's time to prep windows. But here are some tips that will make the job easier.

First, open the window. This may be impossible if paint has dried in the cracks, preventing the sash from sliding up and down. Previous painters may have painted your windows shut. This is a problem if you want to open them for a cooling breeze or need them as emergency exits in case of fire. To fix this, first try pounding the sash frame (*not the muntins,* which are the smaller pieces holding the individual panes) with your palm. If this doesn't work, then slice the paint seal with a utility knife or a window opener, a specialized tool available at hardware stores. Then pound the sash frame again.

When you do open the window, you'll probably find unpainted strips where the upper and lower sashes were concealed. Remove drips and marks from them by scraping and hand sanding. Next, take off all hardware inside and out if you'll be painting both sides: window latch, thermometers, plant hangers, and so on. Tape all screws to corresponding hardware pieces so they won't be lost.

## Working on the Outside

If the window is not protected by a storm window and is peeling badly, heavy sand the window frame and the sash with a disk-sander. *Do not*

*Photo 3-16: Use a disk-sander on a window sash that has peeled badly.*

*sand glass panes or glazing compound.* Then scrape off all loose paint the sander didn't reach, including corners and crevices in and around the sash.

Usually, a storm window's protection will limit the amount of peeling on the window. This lets you get away with little scraping, or none at all. But if you discover peeling on a window protected by a storm window, consider that it will be largely hidden by the storm; you shouldn't spend time meticulously hand sanding rough paint edges when a good scraping to remove all loose paint is adequate.

Replace the glazing compound if necessary. Glazing compound is the putty on the outside of the sash that keeps out the weather. The compound conceals small steel triangles called glazier points. Over time, glazing compound gradually hardens and separates from the sash. Check the condition of the compound before painting. Replace it, as explained below, if it is brittle, curling, or chipped. Hairline cracks in tightly adhering compound are tolerable and may be painted over.

## Glazing Technique

Replace glazing compound only after you've finished all other prep work or can re-install storm windows. Fresh compound is a magnet for dust and paint chips, especially during disk-sanding.

**STEP 1.** To remove the old glazing compound, use the point of a molding scraper. Don't be timid. A ginger touch will not remove all the bad compound from the sash, and window panes are stronger than you might imagine; still, you should wear goggles. If the molding scraper isn't getting all the glazing off the sash, slip a putty knife under the glazing and pry upward.

**STEP 2.** After all loose glazing compound is removed, dust the sash. An old 4-inch paintbrush is ideal. Remember to clean out sash tracks, window sills, and trenches.

**STEP 3.** Replace missing glazier points (the small metal slivers that hold the glass to the sash). Remember that glazing compound only seals out weather; glazier points keep the glass from falling out of the sash. Points should be set into the sash every 4 inches. Push them in flush with the glass, using a putty knife. There should not by any play between the points and the glass.

**STEP 4.** Take a fistful of glazing compound and squeeze it in both hands until it is pliable

*Photo 3-17: Use a molding scraper and putty knife to clear away old glazing compound.*

*Photo 3-18: Press the glazing compound firmly into the sash. It should stand about ⅜ inch high against the glass.*

*Photo 3-19: Angle the putty knife as shown, and draw it across the sash. Press the knife firmly against the sash and glass at all times.*

enough to use with ease but not so gooey that it sticks to your fingertips and putty knife. A lump of hard glazing compound may be left in the sun for a few minutes to soften; a lump of gooey compound may be placed in the refrigerator or in a shady spot to harden.

**STEP 5.** Tear off a small bit of compound and press it into the ledge in the sash. Overlap individual applications so that there are no thin spots.

**STEP 6.** Wipe your hands clean (your pants will do just fine). Press a stiff-bladed putty knife into a sash corner so that it touches the glass, tilt the

blade to roughly a 30-degree angle to the glass, and pull the knife to smooth the compound. Keep the knife pressed against both the glass and sash, as shown in Photo 3-19. This works best using two hands—one pushes the near edge of the blade down on the sash, and the other pushes the far edge of the blade against the glass.

**STEP 7.** When you reach the opposite corner, drag the blade away from the glass while keeping it pressed on the sash at an angle. Otherwise, the blade will pull the compound right off the sash. The compound should be ⅜ inch high against the glass.

*Photo 3-20: Carefully pull away excess glazing compound with your free hand.*

**STEP 8.** Pull away the excess compound with your free hand as you use the putty knife to slice it off against the glass.

**STEP 9.** Gently glide your index finger along the compound in the *opposite direction of the blade's movement*. The compound should be flush with the sash and the glass.

**STEP 10.** Let the glazing compound set for 1 or 2 weeks before painting so that it can develop a semi-hard skin.

*Photo 3-21: Smooth the bead of glazing compound by moving your finger in the opposite direction that you moved the putty knife.*

## Working on the Inside

To scrape the interior side of a window, use a molding scraper and a putty knife. Hand sand all rough paint edges. Make the sandpaper stiffer by folding it into quarters, and sand away.

Sanding serves both to rough up glossy surfaces in anticipation of the new paint and to remove surface irregularities. Take extra care to feather out paint edges that would show through the final coat of paint.

## Finishing Up, Inside and Out

Scrape out the window trench—the slot in the sill that receives the lower sash when the window is closed. Trenches peel like crazy because water settles there. Use a molding scraper and a putty knife.

After all scraping and sanding is complete, clean dirt, dried paint chips, and debris from the sash and frame. Use the molding scraper to lift pieces of paint out of the trench, and a vacuum cleaner to remove the smallest chips and shavings.

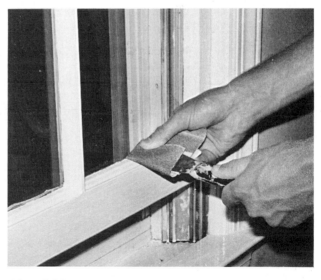

*Photo 3-22: To sand tight corners, place the sandpaper over the blade of a putty knife.*

# CHAPTER 4

# *Paint Problems*

Paint peels for a variety of reasons. Before you paint, you should first figure out why an area is peeling. Once you identify the *cause* of peeling, you can eliminate it and thus ensure that your next coat of paint will last long into the future.

## Blisters

Blisters are domelike protrusions in the paint coat, something like blisters in human skin. They are caused by water that is caught between the paint and the wood. When the water expands, the paint skin is forced off the wood.

There are several ways in which water may be trapped. The paint may have dried too quickly. Painting in the sun or on a hot surface causes the elements in the paint to heat up, and its ingredients may separate and vaporize, creating small vapor pockets. These pockets reduce the paint's ability to adhere to the surface.

Moisture may penetrate the wood from the other side. Bathrooms, interior water pipes, and leaky gutters are possible sources. Moisture passes through the wood and becomes trapped beneath the paint layer, causing blisters. Both latex and oil paints are vulnerable.

An oil-based paint tends to blister if used on a moist surface. Oil and water do not mix, and this moisture remains trapped between the surface and the paint. When the moisture vaporizes, it pushes the paint off the surface.

Before painting, remove all sources of moisture. Replace old caulk and weather stripping, see that pipes and gutters are watertight, and seal cracks in the painted surface. To prevent condensation in moist areas such as bathrooms and kitchens, you can install air vents and electric fans to draw moisture out of the house.

When painting, the precautions are straightforward. Do not paint in direct sunlight or on a hot surface, such as an area that has just bathed in hot sun. Allow the surface to cool before painting it.

Of course, surfaces should be *completely* dry before painting. The drying time may be as little as an hour if the surface is in the sunshine, or a day or more if the surface is shaded. This is a judgment call, so it's best to err on the conservative side.

## Alligatoring

True to its name, this condition looks like the skin of an alligator. Paint contracts, flakes, and falls off in rectangular chips. Watch for the gradual growth of small vertical and horizontal cracks in the dried paint. These are often the harbinger of alligatoring. Alligatoring is most common on older homes because of the thicker oil paints that were once used.

There are three conditions that favor this problem. First, it is apt to strike when glossy paint is applied over a glossy surface. That's because the glossy surface is so smooth that the new coat of paint has trouble gripping it. This allows the new paint coat to shift back and forth, causing it to crack and fracture. Prevent the problem by lightly hand sanding glossy surfaces with 50-grit sandpaper.

Alligatoring also may result if a second coat was applied before the first one dried completely. The second coat of paint cuts off the airflow to the first coat and keeps it from drying. This still-soft first coat then expands and contracts with temperature changes, cracking the upper layer. So, allow each coat of paint to dry completely before repainting. That takes from 4 to 8 hours for latex paints and 24 to 48 hours for oil paints, depending on factors such as humidity, temperature, and exposure to sunlight. You can eyeball a painted surface for dryness by looking for varying shades of paint; dry paint will be a uniform shade. Press a fingernail into wet-looking spots: if the paint is still sticky and pliable, allow more drying time.

Third, paint may alligator if applied too thickly. To prevent this, be sure that each coat is brushed on evenly.

## Cracks

Cracks begin as barely noticeable splits in the coat of paint, then become longer and wider. The process may continue until the paint alligators or begins to curl off the surface. On wooden surfaces, cracks usually run with the wood grain.

The natural expansion and contraction of wood can lead to cracking. When its fibers absorb water, the wood expands like a sponge; when the water is given up, the wood contracts. Green, unseasoned wood is especially vulnerable. This movement pulls the paint apart and creates cracks. Movement is also a problem on surfaces that are flexed, such as garage doors.

Make sure wooden surfaces are kept fully painted, stained, or otherwise protected from water. Use kiln-dried lumber when building and renovating, rather than green wood. There is little you can do to prevent cracking caused by motion stress, other than fully stripping the surface and repainting with a high-quality paint.

Cracks also occur because paint loses its elasticity with time. Even though I say paint "dries" within 48 hours at most, paint does not completely dry for months or even years after application, because it is formulated to retain a degree of elasticity that will resist many stresses. As this flexibility is lost, cracking may appear. There is nothing you can do to increase a particular paint's elasticity.

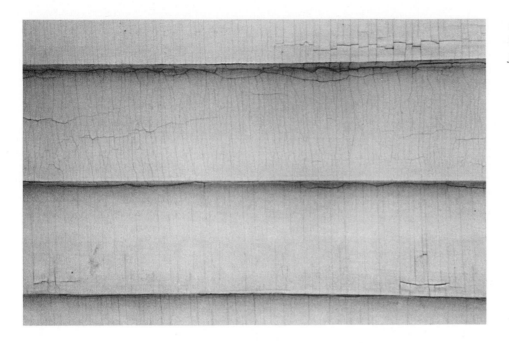

*Photo 4-1: Cracking paint may be caused by a number of factors.*

Thus, the only prevention is to prepare the surface well and to use a top-quality paint. An inferior paint may encourage cracking.

## Flaking and Peeling

Flaking and peeling are catchall descriptions for paint problems. They may be caused by any of the reasons mentioned above: moisture, brittle paint, sunlight exposure, uneven thickness, and so forth. Pay attention to these factors and you will minimize your chances of peeling and flaking.

## Peeling on Brick

Paint may blister and flake on brick for a few reasons. Chemical reactions between the brick and the mortar produce mineral crystals that can push paint off the brick. To prevent this, wash the minerals from unpainted brick with a solution of 15 percent muriatic acid and 85 percent warm water. This acid solution can burn your skin and damage your eyes, so wear rubber gloves and goggles when washing. For painted brick, wash with TSP and bleach (see Chapter 2). Allow the brick to dry, scrape off loose and peeling paint, then repaint: first spot paint the scraped areas, then paint the entire wall.

Trapped moisture may push against the paint and loosen its grip on the brick. Simply be certain that the surface is dry and cool when painting. Moisture may be seeping through a chink in the masonry from the other side, so check for its source on the inside of the house. Also examine gutters and downspouts for leaks.

If the brick or mortar is deteriorating, the paint will surely fall apart as well. You can tell if you have a problem if the backsides of the paint chips are choked with mortar and brick. The wall may have to be repointed with mortar or rebuilt. Contact a mason if this goes beyond your skills.

## Sags and Drips

A sag is a wavy, horizontal line of excess paint. Drips are simply drops of paint headed downward. Both are the result of sloppy workmanship and putting on too much paint. Check your work 15 minutes or so after you apply the paint and use a brush to smooth out any flaws before they dry. Sags and drips are the trademarks of a lazy painter.

## Nail Head Stains

Rusting nail heads may cause reddish brown, circular discolorations on the paint surface. Use

*Photos 4-2, 4-3, and 4-4: Flaking and peeling are often the consequence of using a poor-quality paint. Another cause is dampness from leaking rain gutters and shade trees close to the house.*

rustproof, galvanized nails in visible areas. Finish nails—those with heads only slightly wider than the shank—should be hammered below the surface with a pencillike tool called a countersink. Then fill the holes with caulk or putty. Nails that are not countersunk have more of a chance to come in contact with moisture and thus to rust. Common nails—nails that have wide heads and cannot be countersunk—should be hammered until the heads are flush with the wood surface, then painted.

Rusting nail heads can be sanded to bare metal, then dabbed within 1 hour, preferably with a rust-inhibitive paint. When this paint has dried, apply the finish coat.

## Lap Marks

Lap marks are spots that are slightly different shades than the rest of the painted or stained surface. They spoil the color and sheen consistency of an otherwise good job. They are a particular problem with oil stain, although you can also get lap marks of sorts (called "uneven gloss") when using high-gloss paints. (Latex paint does not leave lap marks even if haphazardly applied.)

Lap marks most often occur when stain is only partially applied over a surface. For example, picture yourself staining a long board. You're halfway done staining it, but it's lunchtime and so you stop staining to eat. An hour later you resume staining. A lap mark will appear at the last spot you stained before lunch. The remedy is to not take a pause from staining until you bring the stain to a visual break in the siding or shingles—a seam, a joint, a split, or the end of a wooden piece. When you resume working from that break, be careful not to get any stain on the finished side of the break, or the overlapped area will look shiny and as if it were a different color.

Another cause of lap marks is an uneven application; thicker stain will dry more slowly, creating a slightly different tone and sheen. Be careful to apply stain evenly.

A third possibility is that a change in surface texture will show up as a lap mark, because rougher boards absorb more paint or stain. When one coat does not provide enough pigment to give a consistent color across an area, apply a second coat.

Should this fail to work, sand down the rough wood and start over.

## Chalking

Chalk is a dry and usually whitish powder that appears on flat (nongloss) paint over time. In simple terms, as paint deteriorates, it wears off the surface in the form of chalk. Chalking actually has a benefit—during rainstorms, it helps to carry away dirt from the paint surface, leaving the house looking fresh and clean. Chalk is a problem only when it is excessive: it dulls the paint's color and can discolor lower boards and brick. You cannot stop chalking once it begins, but you can safely paint over chalking surfaces. First, wash the wall with TSP and water to remove excess chalk, and let it dry. Then repaint with a low-chalking paint; you can use antichalking flat paints or glossy paints.

## Mildew

Mildew is a fungus that grows in, under, and on top of paint and stain. It feeds on organic substances in paint and stain, and given the right environmental conditions of moisture and shade, it will continue growing until entire walls and ceilings are blackened. Mildew ruins color tones and can cause unpleasant odors.

From a distance, mildew resembles dirt. Look closely, however, and you can see small lines branching out from tiny circles. A good test for mildew is to put a few drops of household bleach on the discolored area and wait a few minutes. Do not scrub. If the discoloration disappears or fades, then the splotches are mildew; if the splotches are not bleached out, the discoloration is most likely dirt.

Wash the mildewed area with TSP and bleach. I use a fifty-fifty mixture of water and bleach, and add 2 cups of TSP per gallon of solution, which is stronger than the recommendation on the TSP label. This is a potent brew, so use rubber gloves and goggles. Using a dustpan brush, wipe the area with the solution, drenching all affected areas. You need not scrub: the solution will do the work. The bleach kills the mildew and TSP acts as a soap to cleanse the surface. Rinse the area with a garden hose until the runoff is clear, and allow it to dry before painting.

Do not apply paint or stain over mildew. The fungus feeds on ingredients in these finishes, so you can imagine how quickly it can spread if it finds itself sandwiched within layers of food. Once mildew gets under the finish's surface, TSP washes will kill only the surface growth, allowing the underlying mildew again to eat its way to the surface. The only way to stop mildew inside the paint is to sand the surface to bare wood and repaint.

Most exterior paints and stains are mildew resistant. Interior paints formulated for bathrooms and kitchens also contain mildew inhibitors. Paint stores carry vials of mildew preventatives that you can stir into oil or latex paint intended for use in moist, shaded areas.

## Fading

Over time, paint loses its gloss, brilliance, freshness—and appeal. The cause is natural aging, which cannot be prevented. You can try bringing the appearance back with a TSP wash. But the only way to recapture the old shine is to repaint.

## CHAPTER 5

# Shopping for Paint

Paint is really only a small part of any decorating process. Drapes, carpeting, furniture, and lighting are the true focal points of rooms; outside, the design of the house and its setting are dominant. Because paint is something like background music, you have to choose colors that complement your home.

## Exterior Colors

For exterior use, unassuming color combinations are best. Keep colors soft and simple. Such combinations as orange and blue or purple and yellow look great on a color wheel, and contrast each other wonderfully on an artist's canvas. But I'd venture to say that they would look shocking on your siding and trim. The trick when painting outdoors is to avoid the dollhouse effect—something that looks shiny and plastic and unreal. Look for colors that are relaxing and easy on the eyes.

The architectural style of a home often can be a guide in making color choices. A Cape Cod saltbox looks its most rustic with naturally weathered shingles and white trim. A New England colonial can be painted a variety of dull, flat colors to good advantage—dark red, brown, grey, pale white, and forest green—along with trim painted glossy light grey, white, or cream. Barns look best when painted red or white or allowed to naturally weather. Brick houses are very becoming when painted white or not painted at all. Concrete walls and foundations wear most every color well. The key here is to complement the architectural style by highlighting the natural tones and textures of the construction materials as well as the hues of the surrounding environment.

The greater the contrast a color creates, the more attention it draws to itself. Some homes have exotic or exciting features that deserve to be highlighted; a distinctive color can draw attention to them. By painting an house all one color, you also can purposefully downplay an uninteresting or outright unattractive feature; this helps to unify the inconsistent design and materials of a house that has acquired various additions over the years.

## Interior Colors

We tend to have traditional ideas about colors for exterior clapboard, shingles, and masonry. Interior surfaces, however, seem to invite color experimentation. That's primarily because most indoor materials are manufactured, and we don't think of them as having to be a certain hue. Things such as drywall, plaster, and decorative wood moldings have no implicit color restrictions. So when choosing interior colors, let your imagination and mood be your principal guides.

Light colors make a room look airy and large; dark colors pull the ceiling down and the walls in. So if you have a small room, you can use pastel blues and creams to stave off the feeling of claustrophobia. Unusually large rooms will feel more intimate if painted a dark burgundy or grey or red—this shrinking effect is very useful when you don't yet have enough furniture for the room!

## Help with Color

For more ideas about the use of color on the exterior and interior walls of your home, consult such magazines as *Interior Design, House Beautiful,* and *Architectural Digest.* I find the following books very helpful when I am trying to decide what the impact of a certain color will be:

Donin, Janet. *Ideal Home Book of Stylish Interiors.* New York: Sterling Publishing Co., 1987.

Editors of House and Garden Magazine. *House and Garden's Best In Decoration.* New York: Random House, 1987.

Innes, Jocasta. *Paint Magic.* New York: Pantheon, 1986.

Niesewand, Nonie and David Stevens. *Conran's Creative Home Design.* Boston: Little, Brown, 1987.

Remember the sun. Natural lighting affects the way colors work. In most of the United States, a room with a southern exposure—that is, its windows face south—gets sunlight all day. A room with a northern exposure rarely gets any direct sunlight through the windows. A southeastern exposure brings in lots of sunlight in the morning, while a western exposure gets afternoon sun and great sunsets. Therefore, a light peach color will look darker in a room with a northern exposure than in one with a southern exposure, and a color that enlivens a bright room may fall short of achieving the same effect in a darker room. Northern rooms typically need lighter colors to compensate for their lack of natural sunlight.

Two-tone color schemes can play visual tricks to your advantage. For example, if you put white paint on the walls and ceilings and grey paint on the ceiling molding, doors, and windows, you set up an optical illusion: the grey makes the white look whiter, while the white makes the grey look darker. Keep this in mind when choosing color schemes.

## Brands of Paint

All painters have their favorite paints. A preference for a specific brand develops over the years as a painter notes how well the paint covers, spreads, dries, and wears. For example, I swear by Pittsburgh Paints and Pittsburgh Rez Stains. Other painters tell me they insist on Benjamin Moore, Devoe, Dutch Boy, Fuller O'Brien, Martin Senour, Pratt & Lambert, or Sherwin Williams. The fact is, we're all correct. It's a matter of trial and error and subjectivity. I do, however, have some suggestions on selecting paint and stain.

As a house painting job approaches, you might experiment with a few brands on smaller tasks, comparing their ease of application, covering power, and durability. Which one feels best when you apply it? Which one seems to smooth out well? Which one covers surface imperfections and discolorations and does not look transparent when dry? Which one is available at all times and comes with great dealer support, such as painting advice and tinting capabilities? Stick with name brands. Companies that specialize in coatings and adhesives have a large investment in their reputations, and go to great lengths to maintain product quality. Consider that painting is a labor-intensive job. Why go through all of that work with a cut-rate paint and risk having to watch the house fade or surface flake in a year's time? An excellent job requires excellent craftsmanship *and* excellent materials.

When buying paint, note that three 1-quart cans cost about as much as a 1-gallon can. Therefore, if you are about to buy three 1-quart cans, buy an entire gallon. For no extra cost, you'll have a single large can that is easier to handle and extra paint available when needed.

Prime wooden surfaces with an oil-based paint only. Oil primers seal wood much better and create a sounder base for the finish coat than do latex paints. And a final coat of oil paint seems to hold up better in regions with great fluctuations in temperature. In recent years, however, latex paints have become much more durable and long-lasting; what's more, environmental regulations have purged oil paints of traditional strengthening compounds such as lead. So, a quality exterior latex paint certainly is a good choice for final coats.

## Take a Look at the Ingredients

All paints are composed of a pigment and a vehicle. The pigment is the substance that gives paint its color; the vehicle carries the pigment, allowing it to be spread and to dry. All paints fall under the categories of either latex or oil-based. Latex, or water-based, paints have a water vehicle, whereas oil-based paints have a vehicle of linseed or another oil. Whether a paint is latex or oil is crucial to understanding the way it spreads, dries, and weathers. See Table 5-1, "Latex Paint vs. Oil Paint."

You'll come across two major items when choosing paint: enamel and alkyd. Enamel paints once were invariably oil-based. Today, however, "enamel" means that the paint, be it latex or oil, dries to a hard, nonporous finish. Enamel finishes range from flat to high gloss. A "flat" enamel is in fact a bit shiny. High-gloss oil enamel is somewhat shinier than high-gloss latex enamel. Alkyd paints are oil-based paints that use synthetically manufac-

TABLE 5-1

## Latex Paint vs. Oil Paint

|  | Latex | Oil |
|---|---|---|
| Application | easier, with brush or roller | tends to create lap marks, drips, and sags because of longer drying time |
| Drying time | 1–4 hours | 24–48 hours |
| Vehicle | safe, nontoxic to inhale | flammable, toxic, mineral-based |
| Liquid used to thin paint | water | paint thinner or turpentine |
| Fumes | harmless | toxic; should not be used indoors without excellent ventilation |
| Cleanup | with warm water | with paint thinner or turpentine |
| Price | less | more |

TABLE 5-2

## Where and When to Apply What

| Coating | Surface | Coat 1 | Coat 2 |
|---|---|---|---|
| Paint | bare wood | primer | paint |
| | painted wood | paint | —— |
| Stain | bare wood | stain | stain |
| | stained wood | stain | (second coat of stain optional) |
| Clear wood preservative (CWP) | bare wood | CWP | CWP |
| | wood previously treated with CWP | CWP | —— |
| | wood previously treated with natural stain | natural stain | CWP |

tured soybean resins rather than linseed resins that occur naturally in plants. (Resins are chemicals that hold together the different ingredients in paint and thus maintain the paint's consistency and integrity through to its dried state.) The use of synthetic resins, such as those derived from soybeans, is now widespread because these resins are less brittle, less expensive, and dry faster.

Either oil or latex paint may be used on shingles, shakes, clapboard, and other wooden surfaces. But only latex should be used on brick, concrete, and cinderblock. Refer to Table 5-2, "Where and When to Apply What," to see which coatings go best on various surfaces.

Use like paints on a particular area. Never mix interior paints with exterior paints, or oil with latex. And be careful which paints you apply over existing paint. It's always best to use the same type of paint, for the sake of fewer problems with adhesion. The following combinations are safe, however:

Latex over flat oil
Latex over flat or lightly sanded latex
Latex over oil primer
Oil over flat latex
Oil over flat or lightly sanded oil

Do not paint over glossy surfaces unless they have been lightly sanded by hand. The rough surface allows the new coat of paint to adhere to the surface.

Here is a general guideline on where to use paints of various levels of glossiness. Flat paint is typically applied to walls and ceilings (other than bathrooms, kitchens, and other areas exposed to moisture), shutters, sidings, and trim boards. Semi-gloss paint is suited to bathroom and kitchen ceilings and walls, shutters, trim boards, doors, windows, and moldings. And glossy enamels work well on bathroom and kitchen ceilings and walls, trim boards, doors, and moldings.

## Other Finishes

The clear finishes described below—polyurethane, shellac, lacquer, and varnish—should never be applied to siding or trim. Preservatives may be applied to bare (unstained or unpainted) siding and trim. Do not use any of these over paint or solid or semi-solid stain. Nor should paint or stain be applied over them, unless the clear finish has been completely stripped.

TABLE 5-3

## Interior Coating Choices

| Location | Oil Paint | | | | Latex Paint | | |
|---|---|---|---|---|---|---|---|
| | High-gloss | Semi-gloss | Flat | Primer | Semi-gloss | Flat | Sealer |
| **Drywall** | | | | | | | |
| General use | | | ● | | | ● | |
| Damp areas (kitchen, bath) | | ● | | ● | ● | | |
| Preparation for wallpaper | | | ● | | | | ● |
| **Plaster** | | | | | | | |
| General use | | | ● | | | ● | |
| Damp areas (kitchen, bath) | ● | ● | | ● | ● | | |
| Preparation for wallpaper | | | ● | | | | ● |
| Trim molding, doors, windows | ● | ● | ● | ● | ● | ● | |
| Radiators, metal ducts | | ● | ● | ● | | ● | |
| Wood floors, steps | ● | ● | ● | ● | ● | ● | |

### Wood Preservatives

Clear wood preservatives (made with penta-chlorophenol or tetrachlorophenol) provide moisture and fungus protection for wood siding while allowing the wood to weather naturally. Preservatives are not pigmented wood stains, and they darken wood only slightly. Use them if you wish to seal bare or new wood from weather without losing its rough-cut, rustic look. Perhaps the most important quality of a preservative is the degree to which it penetrates the wood: the greater the penetration, the greater the protection.

### Polyurethane

Polyurethane is a synthetic, plastic varnish that dries to a clear, hard, nonporous film. It is ideal for protecting heavily traveled areas such as floors, thresholds, and steps while letting the wood show through. You may apply polyurethane over bare wood or over natural wood stains. As a rule of thumb, use polyurethane instead of shellac when durability and a clear finish are the major priorities. Polyurethane may give the surface a slight amber tint because of the resins in the ingredients. It is available in a variety of sheens. Do not use it on

TABLE 5-4

## Exterior Coating Choices

| Location | Oil Paint | | | | Latex Paint | | | Stain | | Coatings and Preservatives | |
|---|---|---|---|---|---|---|---|---|---|---|---|
| | High-gloss | Semi-gloss | Flat | Primer | Semi-gloss | Flat | Sealer | Solid, semi-solid | Natural wood | Clear (nonpigmented) | Polyurethanes and Shellacs |
| Wood siding | | | ● | ● | | ● | | ● | | ● | |
| Wood trim | ● | ● | ● | ● | ● | ● | | ● | | ● | |
| Wood shutters | ● | ● | ● | ● | ● | ● | | ● | | ● | |
| Wood doors | ● | ● | ● | ● | ● | ● | | ● | ● | ● | ● |
| Wood window sash | ● | ● | ● | ● | ● | ● | | ● | ● | ● | |
| Concrete, brick | | | | | | ● | ● | | | | |
| Wood, aluminum gutters | ● | ● | ● | ● | ● | ● | | ● | | | |
| Wood floors, steps | ● | ● | ● | ● | | ● | | ● | ● | ● | ● |

metal, plastic, masonry, drywall, or other nonporous surfaces. Polyurethane is thinned with mineral spirits and should be applied with a brush or roller.

### Shellac

Shellac is composed of natural resins and dries to a hard, transparent finish. Use it only on wood and other porous surfaces. Shellac, like polyurethane, is used to protect wood from moisture and physical abrasion, but it is less durable. It is suited to surfaces not subjected to heavy, repeated abrasion, such as doors and cabinets. Relative to polyurethane, shellac is less expensive, more brittle, and dries faster. It is thinned with denatured alcohol and should be applied with a brush.

### Lacquers and Varnishes

For most homeowners, polyurethane and shellac meet every need. But if you are looking for a special sheen for a special surface, ask your paint dealer if lacquer or varnish would be preferable. The principal difference between lacquer and varnish is drying time: lacquers dry very quickly, often in 20 to 30 minutes, which makes them ideal as a spray-can product to keep metals such as brass from tarnishing. Varnish dries in approximately 4 hours, and so may be applied with a brush. Neither should be used on floors.

### Interior Stains

Your hardware store will have a large assortment of wood stains (for fine wood, floors, and furniture) that add a tint—such as shades of redwood, walnut, maple, oak, or rosewood—while letting the wood grain show through. These are oil-based products similar to semi-solid and solid wood stains, but with less pigment.

### Exterior Stains

You have two choices in exterior siding stain: solid stain and semi-solid stain. These terms refer to levels of color pigment: semi-solid stains tint the surface but do not hide the wood grain; solid stains have more pigment and give the siding a finish that looks more like paint. Because of their higher pigment content, solid stains hold their color longer and are slower to fade under sun and rain. You apply these stains just like paint: with a brush and a bucket, using the brushing techniques noted in this book.

When staining siding and trim, use only oil-based stains. Because your goal is to protect the wood from water and rot, oil stain is the only effective solution. Oil repels water. Once an oil film is placed over a surface, the film becomes a water-resistant shield. Latex stains, on the other hand, have a water-based vehicle and thus contain no oil to repel water, making it easy for moisture to seep through. Furthermore, once a latex stain has been applied, future oil stain applications won't completely penetrate to the underlying wood.

### Latex Sealers

If you are going to hang wallpaper on new drywall, the surface must be "sized," or sealed, with a latex sealer. It helps the wallpaper stick and yet will make the wallpaper easier to remove in the future.

# CHAPTER 6

# Brushes and Rollers

A paint job depends as much on the quality of the brush and roller as it does on the quality of the paint. How do you determine the quality of a brush or roller? It comes down to feel and price. Even with no painting experience, you can tell the better brush just by holding it in your hand, dragging it back and forth along your palm, and caressing its bristles with your fingers. The better roller has a fuller nap that you can feel with your fingers, and you will notice its heavier weight and sturdier core. A quick check on price will show you that a brush or roller that feels right will cost two to three times more than the bargains on the rack. Regardless of the size of your project, always use the finest brushes and rollers available.

## Brushes

There is no comparison between first-rate and bargain-basement brushes, in performance or life span. Quality brushes hold more paint, leave a better finish regardless of your skill level, do not shed their bristles, last longer, and make the painting go easier and faster.

Brushes have either natural-hair or nylon bristles. Animal hair is used as bristles for so-called china brushes. Don't be thrown by the term—it's just the traditional name given to natural-hair brushes. Use them with oil paints only, because water ruins the natural fibers. Natural-bristled brushes cost about 40 percent more than those with nylon bristles. Clean them only with paint thinner.

Nylon is used for bristles in latex paintbrushes because it is not affected by the moisture in latex paint. Nylon brushes should be cleaned in water only.

Because stain is much thinner than paint, it is applied with brushes that help to counter the stain's tendency to drip off the brush before you have a chance to apply it. Stain brushes are about 1 inch shorter and 1 inch wider than paintbrushes.

Painting small woodwork requires a delicate touch, so a 2-inch beveled brush is best for control. Exterior siding painting goes quickly with the broad strokes of a 4-inch wall brush.

A brush's bristle mass may be shaped to make certain types of painting easier. A 4-inch-wide flat-edge brush is best for large, flat areas where speed is important—siding, walls, ceilings, steps, and large trim boards. Beveled brushes of 2 and 2½ inches are best for areas where neatness counts, such as window sashes and interior moldings, and when cutting out the edges of walls. Use a 1-inch brush for tiny paint jobs, such as staining a small threshold or touching up a scuff mark.

### Choosing the Best Brush

As I've already mentioned, price and feel are the best benchmarks of quality. At the store, compare a $20 brush with a $7 brush—you'll find that there's little similarity.

The bristle mass should be firmly anchored to the brush handle. Give a tug: an inferior brush will leave bristles in your palm whereas a good brush will lose hardly a bristle or two.

Check the "bounce"—the flex or springiness of the bristles. Wiggle and press the bristles into

*Photo 6-1: From left to right: 5-inch stain brush, 4-inch wall brush, and 2-inch beveled brush.*

*Photo 6-2: Brushes will stiffen if paint is allowed to accumulate near the metal clasping band.*

*Photo 6-3: Use a wire brush to remove dried paint from paintbrushes.*

your palm. The bristles should feel soft, without flexing so much that they become bent or take time to bounce back straight and evenly spread.

Stay away from brushes with bristles shorter than 2 inches. Good brushes of 1 or 2 inches in width have bristle lengths of about 3 inches; 3- to 4-inch-wide brushes have bristle lengths of about 4 inches. The longer the bristles and the thicker the bristle mass, the more paint the brush can hold. That's precisely what you're looking for. Good brushes also have firmly anchored clasping bands and wooden handles.

Beware of multipurpose brushes. Typically, these brushes are lightweight and have plastic handles and thinner bristle masses. They are advertised as ideal tools for any application and cost little, but they give only satisfactory performance in any one category and will not last long. Use them for rough jobs, such as applying chemical paint removers or roofing tar, and discard them after use.

## Brush Care

Brushes should be supple and flexible if they are to apply paint properly. Do not bother to salvage stiff, brittle, or warped brushes. Once paint has dried in and on the bristles, it's exceedingly difficult to remove; discard old brushes and invest in new ones.

Even if they are properly cleaned, brushes will become somewhat stiff over time. This can happen overnight, if all the paint wasn't removed. To restore a salvageable brush, first comb it with a wire brush that has inch-long wires. Brace the paintbrush on a sturdy table edge or paint can, bristles hanging into the air, and comb from the metal clasping band through the bristle mass. Flip the brush and comb the other side. Continue combing until the bristles soften.

To speed the process, you can soak the brush in paint thinner overnight and then shake it out or spin it dry with a brush spinner. The brush spinner device, sold in paint stores, clamps on the handle and twirls the brush to force the water or thinner out of the bristles. Next, comb the brush again. The thinner should have softened the bristles, especially near the clasping band where paint tends to collect. Repeat this only if you've made some progress and the bristles are discernibly softer than before; otherwise, throw out the brush.

*Photo 6-4: Soak brushes used for oil paint in a bucket of thinner. Use a brush spinner, illustrated here, to force the thinner out of the bristles.*

You should begin to clean brushes immediately after use. For latex paints, remove excess paint by pulling the bristles across the inside edge of the paint can several times, turning the brush over after each pull. Then immediately run warm water through the bristles, working the paint out with your fingers. You can use any sink, because latex paint dissolves in water and won't damage stainless steel or porcelain. Flatten the bristles on your palm and wiggle the brush to encourage the paint to flush out. Shake or spin the brush. Then either wrap the brush in foil to keep the bristles from fanning out when drying, or just lay the brush flat if you plan to paint again in a day or so.

For oil paints, remove excess paint as above. Then put the brush, bristles down, in a clean and dry gallon paint bucket. Add paint thinner (it's cheaper than turpentine) until it reaches just below the brush's metal band. After allowing the brush to soak overnight, shake out the brush or spin it with a brush spinner. If you won't be using the brush soon, wrap it in foil for storage. Note that the thinner in the bucket will turn into thin paint after a few days. When you see that your brushes are emerging not as clean as they should, place the thinner in an empty container to throw it away, scrape the sediment from the bottom of the soaking bucket with a stir stick, and refill the bucket with fresh thinner.

Remember that paint thinner and turpentine are flammable, so be careful where you place the open bucket for soaking brushes. Do not smoke when working around these chemicals.

Note that the brush spinner creates a whirlwind of paint thinner mist, so pick out a remote area (nearby woods or behind big bushes is ideal) where you don't care about foliage damage or chance the mist drifting onto your car.

## Rollers

Rollers come in two parts: the roller handle and the sleeve. The sleeve is nothing more than a cardboard cylinder with fuzzy stuff stuck to it. Nap (also called pile) is the fuzzy material on the cardboard tube. It holds the paint on the sleeve much as a sponge holds water. Nap generally comes in three thicknesses: short, medium, and long. The smoother the surface, the shorter the nap you'll need. Interior walls and ceilings are usually fairly smooth, so use a medium nap. Use a short nap when spatter control is critical. Smooth concretes, although somewhat textured—you can feel the bumps when you run your hand over them—can be painted with either medium or long naps. Brick, rough-cut wood, cinderblock, and stucco are rough, pitted surfaces and should be painted with a long nap.

The goal in rolling is to put as much paint on the surface as quickly as possible without leaving roller marks—craters, bubbles, and other surface imperfections. A sleeve with long nap will leave waves and craters on a smooth surface, and a nap that is too short does not carry enough paint to get into the crevices of a rough surface.

Sleeves are replaceable. You can also buy sleeves shaped like doughnuts and cones, and miniatures of the standard 9-inch sleeve. These specialty sleeves are used to paint moldings, corners, and intricate surfaces.

### Choosing the Best Sleeve

Price is a good indicator of sleeve quality. The best sleeve might cost around $4.00 and a bargain sleeve around $1.50. The less expensive sleeve will tend to spit and drip paint on your drop cloth rather than spread it on the wall; it also will be prone to skidding along the wall without turning because the nap is unable to grip the surface. So, spend the four bucks.

Check out the roller in the store. A good sleeve will have a regular consistency through the nap as you roll it in your palm; do the same with a cheap sleeve, and you'll detect small lumps and bumps. The nap should be soft and pliable, but when you roll it in your palm it should not feel loose. Is the nap anchored to the core? Gently tug it. If some pulls off the core now, then it could work itself loose when painting—resulting in a "hairy" paint job. The only way you can get nap off a high-quality sleeve is to rip it, so a soft pinch is all you need to distinguish good from not-so-good.

Does the sleeve feel sturdy, or could you easily break it two? The core strength of a sleeve is indicative of its durability and quality.

### Save a Used Sleeve, or Toss It?

In general, a sleeve is good for a single project and then should be discarded. Trying to squeeze more life out of it is usually pretty messy and ineffective. Fortunately, even the best sleeves are inexpensive, relative to brushes.

You can store a used brush for a month and not notice much change in its ability to hold and smooth paint, but store a used sleeve for a month and you'll find that the nap has developed flat spots and tangles, which cause uneven painting. The nap will also have lost some of its sponginess and, therefore, will hold less paint so that the work goes more slowly. Finally, if the sleeve was not completely cleaned before storing, it will leave a dimple in the paint finish every six.inches. Do not save sleeves for future painting projects.

If you are painting day after day in the same color, however, I recommend that you save your sleeve for the next day's work. Roll the roller on an unpainted wall or newspaper until the sleeve runs out of paint. Tightly wrap the sleeve, still on the handle, in foil. Then pull the sleeve off the handle and fold the foil around the ends to keep out air. The following morning, unwrap the roller, toss out the foil, and get to work.

Do not use the same sleeve for both latex and oil paint. This could result in an uneven surface sheen and peeling problems. But say it's Sunday afternoon, the paint shop is closed, and you have only one sleeve with which to paint one room grey and one room blue. Provided the paints are either both oil or both latex, you can thoroughly clean the sleeve in thinner or running water as you would a brush. Then dry the roller on a brush spinner and begin painting the second room. But beware of the risks. You have a chance of getting off-color streaks. If you apply the lighter color first, you'll be less likely to have this problem.

Once a sleeve has been cleaned like a brush, it may lose some of its ability to hold paint. The nap is apt to tangle and cause spitting. So you may have to rework the sleeve back into shape by rolling it back and forth on a hard surface (the surface you're painting is fine). A minute or two of this will loosen up the nap so that it can better hold paint.

## Foam Painting Pads

Painting pads are foam squares that are cut either in blocks or to resemble paintbrush bristles, and glued to handles. They are inexpensive and at times can produce good results. However, I do not recommend them.

*Photo 6-5: Paint pads are touted as better than brushes, but you may not agree.*

Most professional painters would agree with me. I find that the pads require more time to produce an inferior job. These and a number of other new painting products are the work of manufacturers who hope to capture some of the booming do-it-yourself market by promising an easy way to get the job done. I'm a great proponent of making work easier and more pleasant, as you'll notice throughout this book, but I have found that pads, compared to brushes, don't hold as much paint, don't cover surfaces as thoroughly, and aren't as versatile.

Another mark against pads is that the more tools you have around a painting site, the greater the likelihood that tools will be stepped on or misplaced or lost. A brush and roller will paint everything, but when you paint with pads, you'll still need a brush to take care of certain spots. Furthermore, it takes some practice to develop a feel for a standard brush and roller; because you aren't painting every day, it's best to focus on learning to use these tools well, rather than spread yourself thin by trying to learn other techniques, too.

CHAPTER *7*

# *Ladders and Scaffolding*

Few painting assignments can be undertaken without ladders. Of course, if your house has two stories, you will need an extension ladder to reach high windows and shutters. But even interior painting requires at least a stepladder. Because you will spend lots of time on ladders no matter what you paint, this chapter shows you how to use stepladders, extension ladders, and planks safely and effectively.

## Ladder Safety

Because you'll be above the ground, your first consideration must be safety. Walking a 1-foot-wide scaffolding plank poised 14 feet in the air or bouncing on a 28-foot extension ladder above concrete doesn't sound like much on paper, but I promise that these heights will win your respect on your first ascent. Even the lowly stepladder seems awfully high when an inadvertent shift in body weight threatens to topple you. So before you climb any ladder, you must be aware of the dangers: falling from ladders can cause irreparable damage to your hips, back, neck, and head. The vertical distance itself is irrelevant: we have all read about babies who tumble from fifth-story windows unscathed and homeowners who suffer fatal injuries from slipping off footstools. No matter how high you are off the ground, exercise the highest degree of caution. Always observe the ladder manufacturer's recommendation on proper use as well as your own common sense.

Your equipment should be supremely dependable, and you should be highly familiar with its limitations. For this reason, I suggest you use

*Photo 7-1: If your home rises very far from the ground, you'll need a variety of ladders and platforms to scale its walls.*

your own equipment rather than renting or borrowing it. You never know the history of a ladder that belongs to someone else, and many flaws aren't readily visible: a solid-looking rung may have been weakened when the ladder fell or suffered a strong blow, or the ladder legs may have been bent and later straightened in a way that fatigued the metal. Other dangerous flaws include loose rubber shoes on the ladder feet, poorly anchored hooks on extension ladders, and steps weakened by corrosive liquids such as paint removers.

Use only all-aluminum extension ladders. Today, most extension ladders are manufactured with aluminum, so by purchasing aluminum you are certain to get a strong and new product. Aluminum ladders are also far lighter and easier to handle compared to wooden ladders. Keep in mind that wood is rarely used in extension ladders nowadays, with the exception of specialty ladders used around power lines where weight is a secondary consideration. Therefore, chances are that if you come across a wooden extension ladder, it will be many years old and probably weakened with time and use.

Use only all-aluminum ladder jacks (ladder jacks are hooks that hang on ladder rungs to support a walking plank set between two ladders) for the same strength and weight reasons cited for extension ladders. Do not use jacks made of iron or steel, as these materials show the jacks' age. Because jacks are so critical to safety (jack failure causes the plank and you to fall), they should be brand new and of the highest quality.

Use only all-aluminum planks. Quality scaffolding planks are either 100 percent aluminum or have a plywood walking surface supported by a reinforced aluminum frame—either variety is fine as long as the plank is brand new. Never use wooden planks; not only are wooden planks very heavy and thus more difficult to position on jacks, wooden planks warp over time and can snap in their middles because of invisible weak spots. Wooden planks also don't have end handles for easy carrying up and down ladders.

Stepladders may be either wood, if new, or aluminum. In my opinion, a new wooden stepladder is sturdier and tougher than a new aluminum stepladder; stepladders are an exception to my "aluminum only" rule.

Do not subject ladders, jacks, and planks to undue stress. For example, never let go of a ladder and let it crash to the ground; set it gently on the ground. Do not drop ladder jacks to the ground from their ladder settings; walk them down the ladder. Treat planks with the same respect. By being careful with your equipment, you eliminate the shocks and stresses that could weaken the aluminum's structural integrity.

Extension ladders are sold in three grades according to their ability to support weight: residential, commercial, and industrial. Because you will be placing fairly high stresses on your extension ladders, go with the commercial grade. Residential ladders will support you and a plank but will also bend in their centers when fully extended with a full load. Industrial ladders have more strength than you require, and consequently are harder to move around because of their greater weight.

In shopping for ladders, ladder jacks, and planks, consult your local hardware store or lumberyard to determine what is best for your particular project, and check the yellow pages under "Scaffold."

Some people suggest that homeowners can save money by renting ladders and planks rather than purchasing them. This is really a judgment call on your part: rental equipment ranges in quality from excellent to miserable. I would say that it's fine to rent equipment on which safety does not depend—paint sprayers and disk-sanders, for example. But I feel that purchasing new ladders, jacks, and planks from a reputable dealer is the best insurance you have against equipment failure.

Why all this discussion about ladder quality? Because safety can never be overemphasized. When you are confident that your equipment is the best, you need be concerned only with doing a good job and not whether your ladders will support you one more time.

## Carrying a Ladder

With the ladder resting on the ground, collapse it (make it as short as possible) and engage the ladder hooks. Next, make sure the ladder hooks are pointed away from your body—that is, with the base of the ladder closest to you. Grab the rungs near the fulcrum, or center point, and lift. (You may want to mark the center point with tape.) Although most heavy objects should be lifted by squatting with your legs and keeping your back straight, this method won't work very well here—your knees would get in the way of the ladder, and you would have less balance.

If you grab the ladder by the rungs, you have a great deal of control when walking and are in position to throw up the ladder against the house. This hold is easy on your fingers, too. The ladder is now more an extension of your body than a thing you are carrying.

*(continued on page 88)*

*Photo 7-2: This is the best way to hold an extension ladder when transporting it.*

*Photo 7-3: To throw up the ladder, first stick one of its feet in the ground.*

*Photo 7-4: The lower arm presses down to keep the ladder foot from slipping.*

*Photo 7-5: The throw up: the ladder is pushed up with enough force that the upper arm can be released to grab a lower rung.*

*Photo 7-6: The upper arm now grips a more accessible rung.*

*Photo 7-7: The ladder is stable when straight up, and can be held with one hand.*

*Photo 7-8: To drop the ladder, first allow it to fall sideways.*

*Photo 7-9: Keep up with the midpoint of the ladder as it falls.*

*Photo 7-10: Catch a rung with the free, upper hand.*

*Photo 7-11: Slow the fall of the ladder with both arms.*

*Photo 7-12: The ladder ends up in the horizontal carrying position.*

## Ladder Throw Up

I use this curious-sounding term to describe lifting the ladder to a vertical position, rather than confuse this move with raising the ladder's extension. And, as Photos 7-3 through 7-7 on page 86 show, the term is actually pretty accurate, because you literally throw the ladder up into the air in order to lift it vertically.

Holding the ladder at its midpoint, plant a ladder foot into the ground. In Photo 7-3, my lower arm pulls the ladder down while my upper arm pushes it up. The ladder pivots at my body.

Even though I've planted one ladder foot on the ground, my lower arm continues to press down to prevent the foot from slipping (Photo 7-4).

To get to the point shown in Photo 7-5, I "throw" the ladder a bit—that is, I exert a lot of effort in pulling down with my lower arm and pushing up with my upper arm. The momentum this creates allows me to release my upper grip and, as the ladder becomes vertical, grab a lower, more comfortable rung while my lower arm continues to hold the ladder. Once the ladder is vertical, it can be steadied with just one hand.

## Ladder Drop

How do you get the ladder back down? Essentially, you catch it as it falls, as shown in Photos 7-8 through 7-12 on page 87. I lift the top of the ladder away from the house until the ladder is vertical, then grip a rung below the midpoint. I pull gently to start the ladder falling sideways, to my left (Photo 7-8). I walk with the ladder as it falls, so that the midpoint and my body move together at the same speed (Photo 7-9). I then raise my free hand to catch a rung on the far side of the midpoint (Photo 7-10).

Both arms are now needed to stop the ladder's fall: my right arm pushes down, and my left arm pushes up. Photo 7-12 shows the ladder back in the carrying position.

## Vertical Carry

There will be times when, because of tight corners, trees, or short distances, you will want to carry the ladder vertically without the hassle of dropping it and throwing it back up. With the ladder vertical and resting on the ground, grab it at the second and fifth rungs, or third and sixth rungs

*Photo 7-13: To carry a ladder vertically for short distances, lift with the lower arm and balance with the upper arm.*

(make sure there are two rungs between your hands), with the hooks pointed away from your body. My lower hand curls under the lower rung, and my upper hand curls over the upper rung; my lower arm lifts the ladder up, and my upper arm balances the ladder side to side. When walking toward a new spot, take care not to move so quickly that the ladder top lags behind and causes you to tumble.

## Extending the Upper Section

Extension ladders have a pulley system to raise and collapse the upper section. It's as easy as holding the base with one hand and pulling the rope with the other.

Keep in mind that the ladder should be vertical when you are either raising or collapsing it. Also, quick movements disturb the ladder's balance and you should raise and collapse the extension slowly. Do not let go of the rope when collapsing the ladder—you'd be surprised how the upper section can fall like a guillotine. Keep your fingers and arms away from the extension track, and make sure the ladder hooks are pointed away from your body.

## Two-Person Walk-Up

If the ladder is too long or too heavy for you to lift, perhaps because the the pulley system has jammed and the ladder can't be collapsed, use a partner to help you "walk" it up. With the ladder resting on the ground, position the feet close to the work so that the ladder can be easily guided into its location when vertical. Have your partner stand on both ladder feet while you lift the top of the ladder over your head, as shown in Photo 7-14.

Then walk toward your partner, grabbing each successive rung with locked arms (Photo 7-15). When your partner is able, he reaches down for a rung while you continue walking, as shown in Photo 7-16. He pulls on the rung to help you with the weight of the ladder. Once the ladder is vertical, both of you balance it (Photo 7-17). Because of its height, an extended ladder will be difficult to steady and could easily get away from you and fall, so be extra careful to hold it precisely vertical.

Use the same technique in reverse to drop an extended ladder. But clearly, it's best to collapse the ladder if possible.

## One-Person Walk-Up

This technique is the same as the two-person method, only you use a sturdy shrub or small tree as a surrogate partner to anchor the bottom end. The ladder should be positioned close enough to the work that, once it is up, you can let it fall gently into the spot you need to reach. But even so, the ladder can be tough to balance all by yourself. Remember that the higher a ladder is raised, the more difficult it is to balance and carry vertically.

## Ladder Positioning and Use

The ladder feet should be positioned so that the ladder does not lean to either side. If the ground isn't level, put wood blocks or flagstones under the feet in the air, or dig out the ground with

*Photo 7-14: The two-person walk-up begins with one person lifting and the other anchoring the lower end.*

*Photo 7-15: As the lifting person walks forward, the anchor person bends down, preparing to grab a rung.*

*Photo 7-16: Now both people work to raise the ladder upright.*

*Photo 7-17: Both people should steady the ladder if it is extended.*

your heels and toes. The distance of the ladder feet from the wall should be approximately one-quarter of the distance to the top of the ladder. If the ladder is substantially closer than this, you run the risk of tipping backwards; if it is substantially farther, the feet might slide out from under you.

For the sake of stability, do not rest the lowest rung on top of shrubs, bushes, stumps, or steps so that they support the ladder's weight. Similarly, take care to position the ladder so that its midpoint is not supported on an immovable object such as a chimney outcrop, or the ladder could pivot like a seesaw once you climb above that point. Avoid setting up the ladder on oily, wet, or sandy ground—the feet should rest on a solid, dry surface.

Use rope to anchor an unsteady ladder. For example, if you need to position a ladder to reach a second-story corner window, but ground conditions and the closeness to the edge of the house make you uncomfortable, try this system. Tie a rope to the ladder either at the top or at the spot that seems to have the most sway. Then pull it until taut, and secure the other end to a tree or sturdy structural portion of the house. This is a valuable safety move, provided you have a good anchor for the loose end. There's the story of a man who tied his rope to the family car, and his wife dragged him right off the wall on her way to the store.

Be sure that both ladder hooks are securely connected to the ladder's lower section and that they evenly distribute the extension's weight on the rung. And remember that the hooks should point away from you, whether you are carrying, collapsing, or climbing the ladder. This is a matter of safety: rungs are constructed so that they provide a flat surface when the ladder is leaning against a wall. So, if the ladder is used backwards, the rungs will be slanted, and your feet will be apt to slip off them.

Hold on to the ladder rungs at all times. Take a step up, then grab a rung, step up, then grab a rung. It's very boring, and very safe. Keep your body weight between the ladder legs to keep from tipping or flipping the ladder. If you want to lean out and paint that occasional far piece, rather than taking the time to climb down and reposition the ladder, take this precaution: make certain that you keep your hips inside the ladder legs and extend one of your legs out in the other direction as a

counterbalance, as shown in Photo 7-18. And make no quick movements that could disturb the ladder's balance. Move slowly on your ascents and descents, for the sake of your footing.

Be careful that you are not attached to a cord, rope, or wire that, if pulled, could yank you off the ladder. For example, you might be tempted to tie the sander's extension cord to a belt loop so that the cord won't slip out of your hands and fall to the ground. This works great until someone on the ground trips over the wire, tugging you by your belt loop and perhaps pulling you over.

Be extremely cautious around power lines. Power lines are fully insulated when installed, but over time the insulation can fray. One touch with an extension ladder on a live wire, and it's instant electrocution. So walk around the house before

*Photo 7-18: If you must reach far to one side, counterbalance your weight as shown here, if you feel comfortable with such acrobatics. Better yet, get down and move the ladder.*

raising your first ladder, and drive an orange-flagged stake into the ground beneath the power lines.

Another source of voltage is lightning. Do not paint in threatening weather. Lightning is attracted to both ladders and electric machinery such as spray guns and sanders.

Finally, do not stand on the top platform of a stepladder. It's too easy to lose your balance. Stand on a middle step and hold on to the top platform with a free hand.

These cautions sound so obvious that it seems almost silly to cite them. And yet as soon as people become comfortable on ladders, they become careless on ladders. It's natural to want to get the job done as fast as possible and forget the hazards of what you're doing. That's how accidents happen. So, you may want to review this section halfway through your painting project to remind yourself of safety.

## Jacks-and-Plank System

Here is a simple, inexpensive way to create scaffolding—an elevated work platform, that is—using ladders, ladder jacks, and a plank. It's by far the best setup for the house painter. You can easily raise, lower, and transport it. And it makes elevated jobs safer and easier than if you used ladders alone.

The system is made up of these parts:

Two aluminum ladder jacks
Two commercial-grade, 28-foot aluminum
    extension ladders
One reinforced, 16-foot walking plank

Use quality equipment. I can't overemphasize the importance of this. The same safety and purchase considerations outlined for ladders apply doubly here—which I'm certain you will understand after your first walk across a midair plank. Review the material at the beginning of this chapter before purchasing a plank and jacks.

Make sure the equipment is compatible. A very sturdy plank is not worth much if the ladder jacks supporting it won't hold 300 pounds. The entire system is only as strong as its weakest component.

As when climbing a ladder, be conscious of where you are and what you are doing. The plank is only 1 foot wide and does not forgive errors, so don't become so engrossed with your painting that you take a step back to admire your handiwork.

Keep your toes on the inside edge of the plank at all times. This lets you *feel* the plank through your sneakers without having to glance down, meaning that you can maintain a safe footing without having to look away from your painting. This speeds up the job.

When you're up on the plank, walk with "sea legs." If you've been on a small boat, you know that walking with straight legs is a fast way to fall overboard.

*Photos 7-19 and 7-20: You have better stability on a platform if you scuttle from side to side as shown here.*

To compensate for the deck's movement, old sea dogs walk with a slight bend in their knees. This same bounce in your knees can insulate you from the plank's bending as you walk across it.

Get into the habit of leaning slightly toward the wall when on the plank; when walking along it, place a hand against the wall. Then, if by remote chance you should slip, you will fall toward the wall and not into space.

You can sit, stand, and even lie down on the plank (to work under an eave, for example). Sitting is probably the easiest way to work: preparation and painting seem much less like work, and you're not as apt to lose your balance. To scoot along on the plank while sitting, "crab walk" by lifting your seat with your arms, as shown in Photos 7-19 and 7-20 on page 91.

When sitting down or standing up on the plank, hold the ladder with one arm and the plank (or the wall) with the other. Your balance is most vulnerable when changing positions, so have a tight grip throughout the transition. Always rest your sander, paint bucket, and tools on the plank before changing position so that you have both hands free to hold on.

Keep the plank as level as possible. Ideally, you should be able to put a tennis ball on the plank without it rolling off. Practically speaking, the plank should not be noticeably higher on one side than the other (make sure jacks are placed on corresponding ladder rungs), and it shouldn't be tilted toward or away from the wall. Ground conditions such as heavy bushes and chain link fences, however, hamper ladder positioning. This means jacks cannot always be adjusted to be perfectly perpendicular to the wall, because the ladder feet cannot always be pushed toward or pulled away from the wall. If the plank *must* be tilted, adjust the jacks so that the plank tilts in (so that a tennis ball would roll toward the wall), rather than out.

Do not load the plank beyond its stated weight capacity. I suggest that no more than two people work from it; the rest of the crew (if you're lucky enough to have the help) can work on ground level.

Talk. Whenever you are on the plank with someone else, always announce your movements *and* always wait for confirmation before moving. Your shifting weight will cause the plank to move. If your partner isn't expecting this, even the slightest

*Photos 7-21, 7-22, and 7-23: These photos show how to climb down off the plank without risking your balance. Don't attempt this move with tools in your hand.*

shimmer may confuse him enough to cause him to lose his balance. For example, I would say, "Getting off," and wait to hear, "Okay," before moving.

### Raising the Plank

Photo 7-24 below and Photos 7-25 through 7-27 on page 94 show how two people work together to raise the plank. To lower the plank, use this procedure in reverse.

Position the ladders about 14 feet apart (or about 2 feet less than the length of the plank). Haul up the ladder jacks, as shown in Photo 7-24, and hook them on the ladder rungs. *Positioning is important.* You need to keep two things in mind.

One is the jacks' distance from the wall. Ideally, the end of the jacks should be about 2 feet from the surface being prepped or painted, which means the plank also will be about 2 feet from the surface. A 1-foot gap between the jacks and the wall is too cramped; you wouldn't be able to hang your legs

over the edge without banging your knees against the siding. And a 3-foot gap is too far away; you'd have to reach out so far that you might lose your balance.

The second point to consider in positioning the jacks is your reach—the height you can comfortably reach while standing on that rung. The jacks should be set so that your work is no higher than eye level. This way, you won't have to sacrifice your balance by reaching too far up to work. Also, position the jacks so that you have a full plank's worth of work. For example, if you set the jacks so that the work does not extend above your waist, you are forced to move the system more often, which wastes time.

As your partner climbs up, you feed the plank (Photo 7-25). Be careful you don't feed it so fast that you push him off his ladder. When you come to the end of the plank, begin carrying it up your ladder (Photo 7-26). Your inside hand holds the plank and your outside hand grips the ladder rungs. Your partner then rests his end of the plank on his jack (Photo 7-27). The plank slides along his jack as you continue to climb.

When you reach your jack, lean your chest against the ladder rungs. While continuing to hold the plank with your inside hand, release your grip on the rung, curl your free arm around the outside of the ladder, and grab the plank with your outside hand. Pull the plank across your jack.

Adjust jack settings, if necessary. If the plank is not resting evenly on the jacks, lean against the ladder rungs so that the plank is at your chest and loosen the jack's butterfly nut. Place your palm under the plank and lift. With your other hand, adjust the jack setting. Then place the plank back on the jack and tighten the butterfly nut.

If the ground is irregular, it may be impossible to manipulate the ladders and the jacks so that the plank is perfectly level. Enter a simple device my brother named the Scrupple. It starts with a piece of ¾-inch-thick wood measuring 3 by 5 inches. Hammer two common (flat-head) nails into the wood block just far enough apart for them to straddle the support bar of the jack; these nails prevent the Scrupple from slipping off the support bar. Place the Scrupple on the support bar and under the plank to level the plank. Photos 7-28 and 7-29 on page 95 show how the Scrupple fits on the jack.

*Photo 7-24: To raise the plank, first carry up the jacks.*

*Photo 7-25: The person on the left stays on the ground to support the plank as the other person begins to climb.*

*Photo 7-26: The person on the right rests the plank on a jack, and the other person begins to climb.*

*Photo 7-27: Finally, the person on the left rests the plank on the jack (or in this case, on the door roof).*

## Adjusting the Plank without Dropping the Ladders

After you become comfortable with the scaffolding rig, you will look for ways to minimize moving it. For example, if the jack is hung on the wrong rung or if you want to lower the plank, it's a great bother to carry the plank to the ground, reset the jacks, and put the plank back in place. Below, I describe a method for making these adjustments while up on the ladders. But first, a word of caution. *This maneuver takes strong arms and a bit of practice.* Experiment with the plank and jacks set up only a few feet from the ground before trying the real thing. You won't want to discover that your strength isn't quite what it should be when you're 18 feet in the air and there's no turning back.

To adjust the plank, begin by leaning your chest against the rungs. Using your inside arm, place your palm under the plank and lift. Your partner on the other ladder helps control the plank. The plank should be mid-chest before attempting to move it.

Lift the jack off the ladder rung with your outside arm (your inside arm is now supporting the plank in midair). Lower the jack, and hook its upper curl (the semicircular piece of metal behind the support bar) over the lowest rung you can reach—two or three rungs down. Allow it to fall into place. Grab the plank with your outside hand (you're switching plank hands now), then grab a ladder rung with your inside hand. Descend the ladder, and rest the plank on the jack. Your partner now goes through these steps until the plank is at the desired level.

Keep in mind that as you lower the plank, you will be working farther from the wall—perhaps too far to reach safely. You can adjust your extension ladder's length to bring the plank closer without taking the plank system down, as follows.

Stand on a rung so that the bottom end of the ladder's extension is chest high. Grip the *legs* of the extension—the left leg with your left hand and the right leg with your right hand. Yank the ladder backwards to pull it off the wall momentarily. (You aren't strong enough to pull the ladder so hard that it will fall backwards to the ground!) At the instant the ladder lifts off the wall, push up the extension so that the ladder hooks become disengaged from the rung. With the ladder top back on the wall, yank the ladder backwards again but pull the extension *down* so that the ladder hooks go past the rung they had been resting on.

Next, with the ladder again resting on the wall, step down a rung or two, then repeat the above procedure until you get to a rung that allows the plank to be close enough to the wall. Be sure the ladder hooks are securely set on the new rung.

Finally, descend the ladder, lift its feet off the ground using the vertical carry grip described earlier in this chapter (see Photo 7-13 on page 88), and walk the ladder toward the wall. The plank will be closer to the wall, and you'll approach the ideal one-to-four ratio of distance from wall to ladder height.

*Photo 7-28: The simple gadget with the two nails coming out of it is a Scrupple—a home-made device for leveling a platform.*

*Photo 7-29: Here's how a Scrupple fits on a jack.*

## Plank Setups

The plank can be arranged in a variety of ways to allow you to reach different areas. In the conventional plank setup, one plank simply rests on two ladder jacks, with the ladders about 14 feet apart. Here are a few variations:

**Plank-to-roof.** By resting one end of the plank on a roof ridge, as shown in Photo 7-30, you can avoid potential problems with positioning the ladder. You need to feed the plank to your partner, who should ascend a second ladder (not shown) to the roof to pull it up; then you climb up the first ladder to rest your end on the jack. The Scrupple, described earlier in this chapter (see Photo 7-28), will probably be needed to level the plank.

**Reversed jack.** Photos 7-31 and 7-32 show a forward jack on the left ladder (placed on the roof) and a reversed jack on the right ladder (placed on the ground). You can tell by looking at Photos 7-31 and 7-32 that the second-floor peak would be difficult to reach without this variation of the plank system. Note that the roof ladder is angled so that the top of both legs will rest on the roof; because this requires the ladder feet to be at different heights, you have to nail a piece of wood into the roof under the short leg. Another piece of wood is nailed in just below the other foot to keep it from slipping down the roof's pitch.

This setup is clearly dangerous because of the sheer height involved. You can imagine how hard the patio is at the base of the right ladder (Photo 7-31). Use extreme caution when on the high end of this plank setup.

**Double reversed jacks.** At times it's easiest to reach wall space by reversing both jacks and resting the plank on the outer side of the ladders. Do not hook double-reversed jacks above the second-highest ladder rung, because you'll need to grab the top rung when getting on and off the plank.

When you reverse the jacks while high off the ground, be extra careful. It's trickier to work on this setup because the plank is farther from the wall. There should be no more than two workers on the plank at any time. Move slowly, and always lean toward the wall in case you have to reach out to it for balance. Only one person at a time should climb on or off the plank.

*How* do you get on and off this thing? The only way is to climb over the plank. Take it slowly. This is a demanding move. It can be scary because you'll *feel* as if you're going to fall off. But the only

*Photo 7-30: You may be able to rest one end of the plank on a projecting roof.*

*Photos 7-31 and 7-32: This arrangement of ladders and plank enables you to reach an inaccesible gable.*

*Photos 7-33 and 7-34: This ladder has been anchored by nailing a scrap of plywood to the roof. Another scrap supports the shorter leg.*

*Photo 7-35: The jacks have been placed on the outside of the ladders.*

*Photos 7-36 and 7-37: The lower hook of this ridge jack anchors a ladder for use on a roof.*

way this could happen is if you lose your grip or if you put too much weight on the outside of the plank and flip it back on yourself.

First, climb the ladder until your head bumps the bottom of the plank. Place your materials and equipment on the plank, pushing them toward the center to make room for your climb up and over. While holding on to the rung directly under the plank, step up and reach over to grab the rung directly above the plank. Then let go of the lower rung, and reach up to grab the above-plank rung with your free hand. Step up one rung. Your stomach should be rubbing against the plank edge, and you'll feel cramped. Lift your inside leg up to the plank, resting the inside of your knee on it, while continuing to hold on to the rung with both hands. It may be more comfortable to put your foot on the plank rather than your knee.

Now just pull yourself up with your arms, rocking forward on your knee and kicking up your other leg behind. You still should be holding the same rung with both hands, with both knees on the plank. You've made it! To get down, simply do this in reverse.

**Ridge jack.** For surer footing on an unusually steep roof, you can lay down the ladder's extension. The extension is kept in place by a ridge jack. One hook of the jack secures a ladder rung, and the other hook goes over the ridge.

## CHAPTER *8*

# *Painting Like a Pro*

Next to putting away the last ladder after painting an entire house, the best part of the project is the act of painting. The dirty and tiresome preparation tasks are behind you, so that you are finally free to begin what you set out to do. Painting may seem to be very straightforward, but this chapter describes the details that can make a paint job outstanding. These tips and techniques will help you paint like a pro.

## Paint Spills and Cleanup

Working with paints and stains means that you will get messy. Sometimes your property will get messy, too. It's fine if *you* get messy, but it's an embarrassment and a potentially expensive mistake if your property gets messy. First, we'll concentrate on cleaning you up.

*Photo 8-1: An example of what distinguishes a great job is an electrical box that is painted without getting splatters on the glass dome. Tape newspapers to the dome to protect it while painting.*

By the end of a solid workday, you will be covered with paint. Latex paint is a piece of cake to remove from skin with soap and water: just jump in the shower. Oil paints and stains, however, cannot be diluted and broken up with water. Paint thinner and turpentine dissolve oil-based products quite well, but are harsh on skin. A better alternative is a product called DL Hand Cleaner. DL is a soft white jelly that removes everything from paint to motor oil to grease. Rub DL into the paint and stain spots on your arms and legs, and wipe it off with a thick towel (after a few days of painting, throw the towel into the clothes washer for a paint-clothes-only washing). Keep plenty of DL with you in the garage and a small container in the bathroom. Your skin is the easiest of all clean-up projects.

Dumping a full bucket of paint on your carpet or walkway, on the other hand, is every self-respecting painter's nightmare. Spilled paint denotes sloppy workmanship and carelessness. Moreover, spilled paint can cause hundreds of dollars worth of damage: imagine dumping a bucket of paint down a carpeted stairwell. Even when you watch your step and carry the paint bucket with both hands, dogs and children step into roller pans and tip buckets over. Here are some ideas for handling such emergencies.

Time is the critical factor. The faster you react, the more paint you can get up. So before you spill paint, have on hand at least two gallons of paint thinner (if you're using oil-based paints or stains), as well as rags, paper towels, and hand cleaner.

Clearly, you don't have the time to drive to the store to get these materials after paint spills. Have everything ready to go, preferably in a "spill box" (a plastic garbage can containing all these things so that you can just grab it and haul everything to the spill site at a moment's notice).

Finally, for all paint spills, be careful not to get paint on the soles of your shoes—you don't want to track paint through or around the house in all the confusion. And don't even think about how much it would cost to replace the carpet or to re-lay the brick. Keep cool and work fast.

## Paint on a Drop Cloth

A drop cloth is intended to catch paint, and that's why I recommend that you use heavy-duty ones. If you spill a lot of paint on a drop cloth, quickly lift it by its four corners. If you are outdoors, run the drop cloth out to the grass. If you are indoors, slide another drop cloth or plastic sheet under the splattered one, then bring a large garbage can alongside and dump the cloth into it. Take the can outside and remove paint from the cloth with a brush. Let the cloth dry in the sun.

*Photo 8-2: Be sure all edges are crisp and neat. The white paint on the sill should be sanded off.*

## Paint on a Carpet

This is the absolute worst place to spill paint. If you are going to be working around a carpet, find a carpet cleaning service that handles spilled paint and will respond immediately upon request. Keep the phone number handy and call them as soon as the paint goes down. As an alternative, find out where you can rent a vacuum carpet washer that cleans with liquid solvents (grocery or hardware stores are likely places). As soon as paint spills, scoop up the pooled paint with your hands and deposit it in a roller pan or other handy container. Wipe your hands off with a dry rag. Then douse a latex spill with warm water, and an oil spill with thinner. Massage the water or thinner into the carpet with your fingers and blot up as much moisture as you can with *clean, fresh* rags. Keep dousing and blotting as long as you can coax more paint out of the carpet. Let the cleaning service take things from there, or use rented cleaning equipment.

If you spill only a few drops on a carpet, pinch the carpet hairs between the blades of two putty knives, then lift to squeeze the paint up and out of the fibers. With your fingertips, work droplets of warm water (latex paint) or hand cleaner (oil paint) into the hairs to thin out the paint spot. Clean your hands, then pinch a paper towel around the wet carpet hairs to blot up as much moisture as possible. Depending on how deep the paint has gone, you may be able to snip off the tops of a few carpet hairs that refuse to come clean.

## Paint on Floors

Immediately use your hands to scoop up as much as paint as possible. Then douse the area with warm water (latex paint) or thinner (oil paint). Wipe up the thinned paint with rags or paper towels. On stone, you may need to use a wire brush to remove paint from cracks and crevices. Continue as long as necessary. On outside surfaces only, such as brick and flagstone walkways, rub dirt into the cleaned-up spill to help camouflage the spot.

## Paint on Clothes

Children and unsuspecting guests are notorious for brushing against freshly painted doors and walls. You can usually remove all of the paint if you work fast. First, check the garment's label to make sure it can be washed in water. Then make sure your hands are clean. If the paint is oil-based, press hand cleaner into the spot from front to back; do not use thinner. If the paint is latex, use warm water instead of hand cleaner. Vigorously rub the spot with your fingertips under running warm water. Press in more hand cleaner if necessary, and keep working the cloth to loosen the paint. Immediately wash the entire garment in a washing machine.

## Paint on Roof Shingles

Spilling a bucket from a high point on the roof spells big trouble. The paint will flow like syrup unless you act quickly. Throw a rag—or even your shirt—at the downhill end of the paint to stop its flow. Then, using the rag or shirt as a dam, scoop up the pooling paint with a brush and deposit it in your bucket. Wipe up the paint with clean rags. Add water (for latex paint) or thinner (for oil paint), *slowly* wiping up the runoff before it passes the lower perimeter of the spill—you do not want a pale white streak running past your bright white paint mark. Keep adding thinner or water and wiping until the spot fades. A stiff scrub brush will help get thinner or water into the rough surface of an asphalt roof. Finally, spray the spot with a flat aerosol spray paint that matches the roof color. This masks the pigment you can't get out of the gritty roof shingles. If your roof is an unusual shade, and the paint spill is huge, you might even choose to replace the discolored shingles.

## Paint on Screens

Paint drips on screens are a sign of uncaring workmanship. Screens can be removed from doors and windows prior to painting, so there is no excuse for getting any paint on door and window screens. Permanent porch screens cannot be removed, so as a preventative measure, completely cover immovable screens with newspaper and masking tape before painting the adjacent siding.

To remove wet paint drips from a screen, dab off excess paint with a paper towel; don't smear it into a clean screen. Then have someone stand on the other side of the screen. Push hand cleaner through the spot. Then press your fingers against the spot. Your partner then wipes off the strained

*Photo 8-3: Use drop cloths to protect and tie back shrubs.*

hand cleaner on his or her side with a clean paper towel. Now, repeat this process from the other side—you wipe off the hand cleaner your partner pushes through the screen. Finally, blow through the spot to force out any residual hand cleaner so that a mark isn't left behind.

Once paint dries on screen, it's there forever. You can try dabbing black paint on dried paint spots, but this is not a very effective mask. So attack drips on screens as soon as possible.

## Drop Cloths and Plastic Tarps

Many people don't bother protecting the surfaces they work over. This is risky—paint will spatter no matter how carefully you work. And no one is immune to accidentally dumping a paint bucket on the floor. Newspapers give a false sense of security, because paint will soak right through them.

True drop cloths are thick sheets of cotton or cotton-blend fabrics, specially treated to resist paint. Many painters get by with old unfitted bed sheets, but drop cloths are the preferred protection where your chances of a major paint spill are greatest, such as when working atop a plank or ladder. They'll also cover more area than individual sheets.

*Photo 8-4: Plastic tarps are inexpensive, but they don't give the security against paint spills that drop cloths provide. Also, they tend to tear if walked on.*

And, you can use them to tie back large bushes and shrubs around the siding.

Bed sheets can be picked up inexpensively at the local Salvation Army. They do not provide the protection of a drop cloth, so don't use them where a paint spill would ruin a carpet. But they do a good job under drying doors and on exterior walkways where paint drops from a nearby ladder may land (but a dropped paint bucket probably would not).

Plastic tarps are available from paint and hardware stores. They're cheap, and after you finish painting you can throw them out. But they are easy to tear, which makes them unsuited for use over abrasive concrete and brick. And tarps do not absorb paint, which means you are more likely to get paint all over the soles of your shoes.

As a general rule, drop cloths are for both interior and exterior use, and plastic tarps are for interior use only. I prefer to use drops and sheets for all painting, indoor and outdoor, but you may safely use tarps to protect cabinets and couches when only roller spatter is likely to strike the tarp and to seal doorways through which paint spatter could reach the next room.

Anything that would be discolored or damaged by paint spills and spatters should be fully covered with drop cloths or plastic tarps. Outdoor examples of what you should cover are: concrete, brick, and stone walkways, as well as steps, iron railings, driveway aprons, and porch floors. Indoors you should cover hardwood floors, carpeting, heavy furniture, and stairs. Portable items such as tables, chairs, and lamps should be moved out of the painting area before laying drop cloths; large pieces such as pianos and cabinets may be left in the room provided they are covered by drops and sheets.

## Masking Tape

Use masking tape frequently, especially when you want a crisp paint line without the trouble of being precise with the brush. Masking tape makes the work go faster, as well as tidier. In Photo 8-5, imagine how hard it would be to paint the siding without accidentally slapping your paintbrush on the roof shingles. By running 3-inch tape on the roof flush to the siding, you can paint right down to the bottom of the siding, and quickly, without worrying about getting paint on the roof.

*Photo 8-5: The 3-inch masking tape keeps paint from touching the shingles, allowing you to paint faster. Remove the tape after the paint has dried.*

Masking tapes come in a variety of widths, and 1½-inch-wide tape should meet all of your needs, although the tape in the photo is 3-inch. Buy the best masking tape you can, which means the most expensive you can find. The better tapes seal tightly at the edges, which keeps paint from seeping underneath.

Use masking tape only on durable surfaces that will not be damaged by a sticky adhesive (concrete, wood, hearty carpet, tile, and so forth). Wallpaper should not be covered with masking tape: the tape will pull the wallpaper off the wall when removed.

Taping goes faster if you use long strips. The trouble is, long strips are difficult to tear off without creating a tangled mess. Here's a method that works well for me. Hold the roll with your right hand and the tape end with your left. Pull the tape off the roll until your left arm is fully extended, then bite the tape right at the roll with your teeth. Rip the tape at that point, and drop the roll to the ground. Now that your right hand is free, you can take the tape out of your mouth and hold it taut between your hands as you apply it.

Pinch the outside edges—those that will face the surface to be painted—between your thumbs

*Photo 8-6: This baseboard can be painted more quickly because of the protection provided by the tape and plastic tarp. A drop cloth would be more durable and it makes a better barrier in the event of a paint spill.*

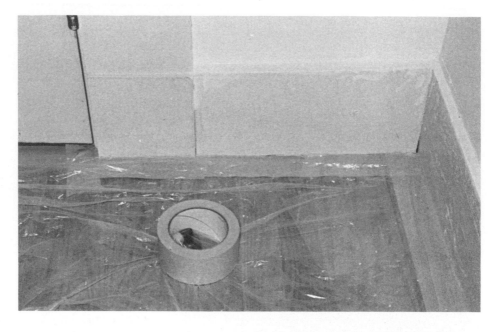

and first two fingers and pull tightly. This causes the middle of the tape to bow outwards. Then press one end of the tape on the surface—this end should stick enough so that you can let go and it won't fall. Then guide the rest of the tape into position by running your fingertips down along the tape. When taping, pay attention to two things: overlap and tight seals. Masking tape must overlap slightly onto the surface that is being painted, so that it will leave an unpainted strip about 1/16 inch wide. Otherwise, you'll stand to get paint on the protected surface. A tight seal is also crucial. If the tape does not lie flat and adhere firmly to the surface, paint will seep underneath, ruining the sharp-cut line you are after. Run your fingers along the length of the tape to make sure that it lies flat along the edge to be protected.

Do not remove tape too soon—or too late. The tape should stay put until the paint becomes tacky (30 minutes for latex paint, 2 hours for oil); otherwise, the still-wet paint could drip into the area you want to protect. On the other hand, if you leave tape on any surface for more than 2 hours in direct sunlight, or 6 hours in shade, the adhesive may come off the paper and stick to the surface being protected. Note that paint is slower to dry on tape and in the space between it and the wall; this means you should carefully pull the tape away at a 45-degree angle to avoid smudges.

*Photo 8-7: Run your fingers down the length of the tape to make certain that paint won't creep under it.*

*Photo 8-8: Use tape to protect hinges, doorknobs, locks, and thresholds.*

*Photo 8-9: Tape doorknobs instead of going through the trouble of removing them.*

Do not bother to tape around easily removed items such as electrical outlet plates, thermometers, plant hangers, and doorknob trim plates. The final result will look much cleaner if you unscrew them. But to save time you should use tape to mask immovable (or hard-to-remove) hardware such as doorknobs, hinges, metal thresholds, garden hose spigots, and locks.

### Painting Tape

Painting tape has a softer adhesive than masking tape and will not damage wallpaper and other surfaces. It is especially useful for masking wallpapered walls when painting the ceiling. For more protection, newspaper can be hung from the painting tape with masking tape. Because painting tape's adhesive is weak, it needs extra pressure to form a tight seal. When you remove the tape after painting, pull it away at a 45-degree angle to prevent it from brushing against the fresh paint.

## How to Handle Paint

Paint comes in gallon and quart containers. You may paint directly from these containers or from separately purchased paint pots. I paint directly from gallon paint buckets whenever possible. This makes life easy. The bucket holds plenty of paint, has a wire loop handle, is discardable, and has a paint track around the rim to control drips down the side. Finally, the bucket comes free with the paint.

I use aluminum pots when staining, because 5-inch-wide stain brushes cannot fit into regular buckets. You can use a pot to hold paint as well, but remember it will be one more thing to clean at the end of the day.

Plastic dishes from margarine spreads and dessert toppings are handy when you touch up small areas and don't need much paint. Still smaller are paint bucket lids holding only a brushful or

*Photo 8-10: To paint the ceiling over wallpaper, run painting tape along the top of the wall. Then hang newspaper from the painting tape with masking tape.*

*Photo 8-11: Be sure to pull the tape sharply away from the freshly painted ceiling.*

## E Q U I P M E N T **&** M A T E R I A L S

### Painting Indoors

2½-inch beveled brush

Doughnut roller (optional)

Drop cloths

Extension pole for roller handle

Lamps and aluminum foil

Masking and painting tapes

Paint

Paint thinner

Roller pan

Roller sleeve and handle

Screwdrivers and scrapers

Stir sticks

Stepladder

two of paint. Use any type of container that seems right for the job: store-bought, Cool-Whip, Tupperware. Simply be certain that the container is clean, dry, and watertight, with a strong bottom.

Always use a bona fide store-bought pothook when hanging a bucket or paint pot! I've seen painters use a wire coat hanger, twisted around the bucket's handle and the ladder rung, but this makeshift hook has a fifty-fifty chance of unraveling, which would leave a pretty large paint splash below.

I never entirely trust the wire handle on a gallon bucket or pot. So, I suggest that you carry the bucket with two hands—one holding the handle and the other supporting the bottom of the bucket—when you transport paint over concrete, brick, or flooring.

*Photo 8-12: Invest a few cents in a bona fide pothook, rather than risk a paint spill by making your own hook.*

## How to Mix Paints and Stains before Use

Have your paint dealer shake all paints and stains (but not polyurethane) before you load them into your car. The pigment will have sunk to the bottom of the bucket during shipping and storage; this is particularly true of stains.

In addition, mix the paint or stain just before using it to make doubly sure that the pigment is evenly distributed throughout the vehicle. Otherwise, the color of the surface may not be consistent. It's vital that the paint and stain be smooth (no lumps of pigment lying on the bottom of the bucket) and evenly colored (no circular oil streaks) before you apply them.

First, lay down a heavy drop cloth to catch spills. Use a large flat-head screwdriver to pry the lid off, being careful not bend the lid out of shape so that it cannot be hammered back on.

To mix a few gallons, you need stir sticks and a large 5-gallon plastic mixing bucket, available at paint stores. Stir sticks are the ruler-sized wooden paddles that you are given when you buy paint. Pour 2½ to 3 gallons of paint into the 5-gallon mixing bucket, digging out any residual pigment with a stir stick. Stir until the paint feels and looks smooth. Then pour ⅔ or ¾ of a gallon of paint into the 1-gallon bucket. By not topping off the bucket, you won't spill paint when you carry the bucket.

If you have only a gallon to mix, don't attempt to stir it right in the full bucket! Pour a third of the paint into an empty, clean 1-gallon container, and you'll be able to stir without spills. Pouring paint from a full bucket is tricky. Tip the bucket quickly, or the paint will run down its side; to stop pouring, quickly tip it back up, but only halfway, to a 45-degree angle.

Before hammering the lid back on a can, clear the paint out of the track around the rim with a brush. Lay a drop cloth or newspaper on top of the lip to catch paint spatter, then hammer the lid tight.

## Priming

Priming is a term many homeowners don't understand. It means applying a special paint to bare wood or metal so that subsequent coats of paint adhere better.

Photos 8-12 and 8-13 illustrate priming: only the sanded spots are primed, and the painted shingles are not primed at all. The final coat of paint, of course, covers all of the siding. Therefore, "painting" is really two distinct steps:

■ Step 1 is applying primer paint to bare wood.
■ Step 2 is applying finish coat paint to the whole surface.

If you have sanded anything to bare wood, indoors or outdoors, you must apply a primer before using paint. Why primer instead of regular house paint? Because primer contains less pigment, sinks in better for a more adhesive grip, and dries to a slightly granular texture. This rough surface allows subsequent paint coats to improve their grip on the wall, so that they are less likely to peel in the future.

Primer is always the first coat of paint put on *unpainted* surfaces, and thereafter only paint is

*Photo 8-15: To avoid spraying paint when you hammer the lid back on, cover the can with a cloth or newspaper.*

*Photos 8-13 and 8-14: Pour three individual gallon cans into the 5-gallon bucket for mixing. Then pour the mixed paint back into the gallon cans.*

applied. Use an oil-based primer for bare wood, a rust-inhibitive primer for metal, a transparent masonry sealant for brick and concrete, and a latex sealer for new drywall and plaster.

To repeat, do not prime already-painted surfaces. An existing coat of flat paint provides an adequately rough texture for your new coat to grip; glossy paint should be roughed up in the preparation stage by hand sanding to take the sheen out and to create the tiny ridges and bumps to which the new paint can adhere.

Do not use primer for your finish coat. It lacks the color, sheen, and weathering qualities of paint. Applying primer over paint will not damage a paint job, but neither will it match the longevity of paint. Apply primer just as you apply paint: smooth with the wood grain, and use as much as the surface will hold.

Primer is usually white. This can cause a color consistency problem if your final coat of paint will be a dark color—the final coat may not completely cover the underlying white primer, leaving a streaked and irregular appearance. So, have your primer tinted the approximate color of the final coat. Your paint shop will be able to do this for you.

At this point, you should be seeing the light at the end of the tunnel! All the prep work is complete, you know when to use masking tape and drop cloths, and you understand the difference between priming and painting. It's now time to apply the final coat of paint.

*Photos 8-16 and 8-17: On this house, only the heavy sanded areas have been primed. The shingles that retain their paint are not primed at all.*

## Painting and Staining Tips

Painting a house is not simply a matter of sticking a brush in the bucket and slapping paint on the house. Here are a number of tips that can make the work go more quickly and more neatly. Refer to Chapter 2 for preparation tips.

**Avoid drips.** They are the hallmark of a sloppy painter. Check your work 15 minutes after applying the paint for drips around trim boards, door panels, window sashes, and shutter slats. If you discover a drip and the paint is still wet, simply smooth through the drip with a brush; if the surface is tacky (somewhere between wet and dry;

sticky) allow the wall to dry overnight and then slice off the drip with a putty knife, pushing the knife from *bottom to top*. The drip will still be soft, even though the wall has dried.

**Do not paint in wet weather.** This includes at the crack of dawn as well as right after a rainstorm. You may need to wait until 9:00 or 10:00 A.M. for the morning dew to burn off the siding, depending on the wind and sun. Use your judgment: a touch should tell you if the surface is wet, and you can look for sparkles of moisture on the surface. If in doubt, wait a little longer rather than risk putting on a coat that won't wear well.

**If you're using oil paint, you can paint until the rain falls.** Even violent downpours will not wash away freshly applied oil paints and stains. But you should stop applying latex paint at least 30 minutes before you expect rain, or the paint will be thinned. Keep this in mind when trying to beat an oncoming storm; you don't want your efforts dripping down the front of the house and pooling in the driveway.

**Follow the sun.** As when sanding, try to avoid glare and heat by positioning your work so it is never in direct sunlight. For example, if your house faces west, work in the front in the morning, break for lunch around noon as the sun passes over the roof, then work in the back of the house for the afternoon. Ideally, you should paint in shaded areas recently bathed in sun. This ensures both that the surface is free of moisture and also that the paint will not be dried too quickly (the next time that spot will be sunbaked will be the following morning).

**Protect surfaces that aren't to be painted.** Outdoors, take the time to cover concrete, brick, and stone walkways, and stone walls; indoors, cover floors, carpeting, and heavy furniture that can't be moved out of the way. Use masking and painting tapes to protect anything your brush or roller shouldn't touch. This includes trim and floors. You can place newspaper under drying objects to protect the floor from drips, but you'll need drop cloths to guard against major paint spatters and spills.

**Tie clean rags around the top of the ladder's legs.** This is to avoid scuffing newly painted surfaces, such as the siding, when you are painting trim, scraping windows, or installing shutters.

**To assure color consistency between cans of custom-mixed paint, stir them together in a 5-gallon plastic container.** A drywall compound bucket is perfect, or check a local grocery store for containers that held pickles or potato salad. Mix all stains even if they are off-the-shelf colors. You can add mildewcides during this mixing.

**Carry a molding scraper and putty knife with you while painting.** You may have missed a small spot of peeling paint during preparation or dew may have loosened once-solid paint. When you have the tools with you, you can zip off the peeling paint and paint right over the spot; this saves you a trip down the ladder in search of scrapers.

**Work systematically— from top to bottom, from left to right.** I concentrate on sections of siding or interior wall measuring roughly 8 feet square. This keeps my attention focused, reduces the number of ladder and plank setups, helps prevent lap marks, and makes the job go more quickly. A systematic approach is especially important when applying oil stain, because it helps you to leave wet edges so that lap marks are less apt to ruin the consistent color tone of the job.

**Even though oil paint is less susceptible than stain to lap marks, glossy paint is prone to them over its long drying period.** The more pigment in a stain or paint, the longer you can go before lapping occurs; I call this period a finish's safety zone. Table 8-1 gives a rough guide to how long you can allow paints and stains to dry before lap marks are apt to show. (Latex paints do not leave lap marks.)

**It's easier to avoid lap marks when painting and staining from the ground.** This is because you don't have the time delay caused by repositioning ladders. You shouldn't have to paint only to natural breaks, provided you quickly move on to the next section. If you will need to break for longer than a minute or two between sections, you can rewet the edges with your brush just beforehand.

**Take care of your brushes.** Periodically pull your brush against the inside rim of the bucket to keep the bristles from clogging with paint near the clasping band. If you are taking a break of no longer than 3 hours, here's an easy way to avoid having to clean the brush. Put 2 inches of paint in a bucket, and place the brushes in it to keep the bristles from drying out.

TABLE 8-1

## How Long Will the Edges Stay Wet?

| Oil-based Coating | Safety Zone (min.) |
| --- | --- |
| Flat paint | 10 |
| Glossy paint | 5 |
| Semi-solid stain | 1 |
| Solid stain | 2 |

**Remove the bulbs from any fixtures that you leave on the house.** Nighttime bugs are attracted to lights, so don't give them any incentive to get stuck on your fresh paint. Don't rely on yourself to keep the lights turned off—someone may accidentally turn on a light over the freshly painted garage door, for example, and the next morning you'll discover the paint is blackened with bugs.

**Get the bugs out.** To remove bugs or bristles from a newly painted surface, poke at them with one corner of the bristle mass, and lift the brush off the surface. If you find a bug in tacky paint, let the paint dry completely. Then gently brush off as much of the bug as you can, and dab the mark with paint.

**Let a wall dry completely before evaluating your work.** As paints and stains dry, they look uneven and splotchy. Allow the surface to dry completely before even considering the thought of touching it up.

## Painting Siding

If you have used a brush before, you may find the following explanations a bit too detailed; then again, you may also discover a few new tricks. The technique is the same for shakes and clapboard. Hold the metal clasping band between your fingers and thumb, as shown in Photos 8-14 and 8-15. Why hold the brush in this unconventional way? After all, when you reach for a brush, you simply grab the handle with a handshake. But this grip restricts your ability to move the bristles along the surface because it stiffens your wrist. With the grip shown here, however, the brush is an extension of your wrist rather than a tool you hold, enabling you to swivel and angle the bristles throughout the entire brush stroke without repositioning your body in the process.

In order to keep your muscles from cramping up, which will happen after a while with this brush grip, I suggest you try alternating hands. And, to paint under the lip, you can switch to a handshake grip.

Dip the brush ½ to 1 inch into the paint. As you pull the brush out of the can, drag the bristles against the rim to remove excess paint. Paint the lip first, running the brush against the bristles, as explained in "Painting with and against the Bristles."

Once the lips of a reachable area are painted—

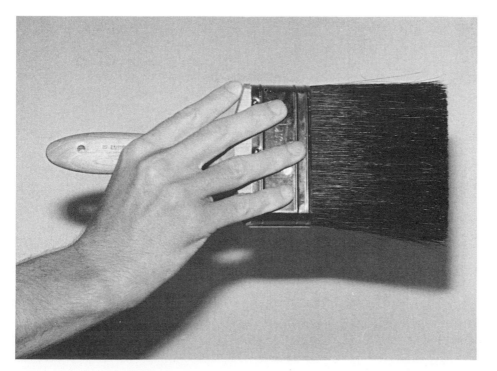

*Photo 8-18: Try this grip when brushing paint on siding.*

*Illustration 8-1: Hold the brush bristles up in order to paint the lips. Once you've done the three lips (as shown here), you're ready to paint the siding or shingles below them.*

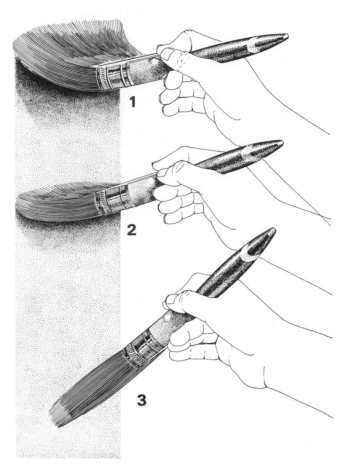

*Illustration 8-2: Feathering with a brush.*

about the three lengths of lips shown in Illustration 8-1—do the surface. For this, you need to get much more paint on the brush. Dip it 2 inches into the paint, while making sure to keep at least 1 inch of clean, paint-free bristle beneath the metal clasping band. Drag the bristles against the inside rim of the can to clear paint from the underside of the bristle mass. Even so, as soon as you pull the brush out of the can, paint will begin to drip. That's as it should be. Remember that the more paint you have on your brush, the faster you can paint.

To keep more paint on the brush, turn the brush parallel to the ground as you pull it from the bucket. This forms a pool of paint on the bristles. Now quickly press the paint-laden side against the siding. The first pass of the brush spreads the paint; the second pass spreads the paint over the same area to keep it from dripping; and subsequent brushing smooths the paint. To make one brushload blend well with the next, you must feather them. Pull the brush from the unpainted area through the just-applied coat of paint into the previously applied coat, where you gradually lift the bristles from the surface.

Finally, smooth out the paint in the direction of the wood grain. That's because the brush leaves small bristle trails in the paint that no painter can eliminate, and these marks are very noticeable if they are running against the grain. On clapboard, the smoothing takes place side to side, because clapboard's grain runs side to side; on shingles, smooth top to bottom.

In time, you'll have to clear paint from the metal band, or else the brush will begin to drip paint uncontrollably from the band. To do this, you can drag the bristles over the paint can rim several times, flipping the brush after each pull. But I prefer to remove the paint by dragging the brush upside down against the siding lip, then flipping the brush to spread the excess paint on the siding. I do this for both sides of the bristles. It

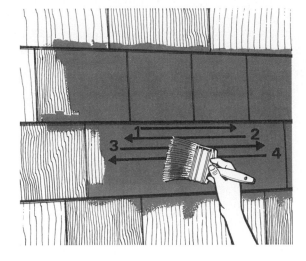

*Illustration 8-3: Draw the brush back and forth across the siding. You're likely to need to make several passes, each spreading paint out over a larger surface. When you see that the paint isn't quite covering, it's time to dip the brush again.*

*Illustration 8-4: Once paint has been spread over shingles with horizontal brush strokes, smooth it with the grain—that is, vertically. Stick the bristle tips under the lip and pull the brush down the width of that shingle.*

saves time by putting paint on the siding, rather than back in the can.

### Brushing Tips

Check for drips and sags 15 minutes after applying paint. Imperfections in either the painting or priming stages cannot be hidden by subsequent coats of paint, so smooth out drips and sags with your brush as soon as you see them. And keep a wet edge. That is, don't allow the first brushful of paint to dry or get tacky before you feather the second brushful of paint into it. It's important to prevent lap marks—the glossy spots created when wet stain and paint is spread over dried stain and paint. To avoid lap marks and uneven gloss, feather just-painted areas into previously painted areas before moving on to the next siding block. When it comes time to put down the brush, stop painting only at natural breaks—trim and siding joints, cracks and splits in wood, corners, the ends of boards, and between shingles. Paint all the way up to the break; it doesn't matter if you go a bit over. Resume painting from that line, but take care to avoid getting paint on the last completely covered board or shingle.

The larger the brush, the faster you paint. I use 4-inch brushes on siding, wide trim boards, windows, doors, and cabinets; I use 2½-inch brushes for cutting out and touching up. I never use smaller sizes, because they really slow down my pace. As you learn to handle a brush, you'll feel comfortable graduating to larger ones.

Angle the brush in the direction it is traveling. If you are pulling the brush left to right, tilt the brush handle toward the right so that the handle passes over the surface before the bristle mass actually paints the area. This helps the paint flow smoothly off the bristle mass.

Wiggle, press, and squish the bristles! Use some force to get that paint on the surface as quickly as possible, especially if the surface is rough or uneven.

With a little practice, it's easy to paint window sashes, doors, shutters, and thin moldings with a 4-inch brush. When you need to reach a tight corner, just swivel the brush so that you're painting with only the tip.

## Brick, Concrete, and Masonry

The first thing that should pop into your head when you need to paint these surfaces is—roller. A roller with a heavy nap is the fastest and easiest way to paint these rough and crevice-riddled surfaces.

Whether you are painting a brick wall or a concrete floor, you can make the work easier by attaching the roller to an extension handle. The best part about rolling these surfaces is that you do not have any grain to follow, unlike wood. So, you can roll the paint diagonally, side to side, then up and down—whatever is fastest. However, be sure the final strokes are all in one direction so that you avoid crisscross lines.

Just keep these basics in mind. Paint top to bottom and side to side, so that you don't skip an area. Use lots of latex paint on a thick-nap roller.

## Exterior Stain

It may be that your house is not painted at all. The siding and perhaps even the trim could be coated with stain. You may have difficulty telling the difference between the two, so here are a couple of clues.

Check the basement or garage for old stain buckets. Or, check the siding. If it shows any signs of peeling, then you can be confident that the stuff is paint. If there is no peeling, examine the siding closely: paint is a coating that fills in the wood grain to make a flat surface; stain does not have the thickness of paint, and thus allows the texture of the wood to be seen and felt. A sure-fire way to confirm this diagnosis is to take a small piece of the siding wood to the paint shop and ask the owner.

Why would you want to apply stain instead of paint? Because stain does not peel. As the chapters on preparation make clear, there is a lot of work involved in readying a painted surface for a new coat of paint: heavy sanding, fine sanding, washing, and priming. But old stain doesn't peel, and it requires no sanding. You just wash the surface and apply fresh stain. What's more, stain is much easier to apply than paint, so you finish faster. And because stain is available in a great variety of colors, chances are you can find the shades you want.

You can apply stain to new wood, to siding that has been sanded to bare wood, and to siding that previously was coated with stain or sealed with clear preservative. If your home has severe peeling problems, consider hiring professionals to sand or sandblast the siding and trim; then you can do the relatively easy work of applying two coats of stain.

Before shopping for stain, consider your alternatives: clear wood preservatives, semi-solid stains, and solid stains. Clear wood preservatives contain no color pigments and are used primarily to protect wood from moisture while retaining the wood's natural color and texture. A semi-solid stain is a good choice when you want to give siding some color without masking the wood grain and texture. It has less color pigment than a solid stain, and fades more quickly. Solid stains are best when you want to give siding a strong dose of color, while not covering the grain as completely as paint. You can't count on solid stain to have a consistent color tone, however, if applied over rough siding: variations in surface texture will cause noticeable (but not flagrant) differences in hue. By spot sanding rough areas, however, you can minimize color variations.

Do you have to prime bare wood before staining? Absolutely not! Priming involves applying a thinned-out coat of paint to bare wood, and this coat would prevent the stain from penetrating the wood surface. And you should not apply a thinned-out coat of stain to bare or new wood. Just apply two coats of stain right out of the can. The first coat of stain will sink into the bare wood, and the second coat will bring color consistency to your work. Under no circumstances should you alter the stain (for example, trying to thin it or thicken it).

In brief, stain is a pleasure. Preparation is a snap, and application is fast and easy. The only disadvantage is that one coat of stain generally has a shorter life than one coat of paint: stain fades more quickly, so it has to be reapplied more often to get rid of that washed-out look. A single coat of stain typically lasts 2 or 3 years before fading, whereas a single coat of paint on a properly prepped surface looks good after 4 or 5 years. You can compensate for this color fading problem by applying two coats of solid stain.

You brush and roll stain the same way you apply paint. But be aware of these rules:

**You can apply paint over stain, but never stain over paint.** Paint sticks to dried stain, but the hard surface of paint is not porous enough to let stain sink in and get a grip on the wood, literally causing the stain to fall off the wall.

**You can mix stains of the same brand or type to create your own colors (just as you**

can mix paints), **but never mix paint and stain together.** Even oil paint and oil stain are not compatible, and will not form a durable coating.

**Keep wet edges at all times in order to avoid lap marks.** The full explanation of this risk is given below.

### Watch Out for Lap Marks

Lap marks can be the villain of any stain job. The principal cause of these shiny or off-color spots is applying stain over areas that have already dried. Another cause is a varying degree of porousness within the same boards.

You cannot see lap marks until the stain has dried, so there's no way to correct them other than completely restaining the area. You could finish up a day's worth of staining, go to sleep, and the next morning find lap marks on what you thought was a great job. Fortunately, lap marks are easy to avoid if you employ all of the following precautions.

Apply two coats of stain. After the first coat of stain, the wood is clogged with pigment and cannot absorb as much of the second coat of stain; this means the second coat dries more slowly, decreasing the likelihood that you will smooth wet stain over dry.

Stain no more than three rows of shingles, shakes, or clapboard at one time. This makes it unlikely that the stain edge will dry before you extend it with a new brushful.

Stop the brush at a break in the siding—the end of a board, or the edge of a shingle. This allows you to knock off for lunch or even quit for the day without leaving a lap mark.

It helps to apply stain quickly. The stuff will drip and spatter and run down your arm and make a mess out of your brushes, but that's good! Because stain is thinner than paint, you need to get it out of the paint pot and onto the siding as quickly as you can. The stain will drip down the board like crazy, so move the brush back and forth quickly to keep as much of the stain on the siding as possible. After a bit of practice, you'll be able to spread a brushful without losing a drop of it to gravity.

Stir the stain periodically. Pigment and vehicle separate fairly quickly. If you do not draw a stir stick through the stain once in a while, the pigment will settle to the bottom of the pot and the stain will look progressively paler on the siding.

## Painting with and against the Bristles

Paint *with* the bristles when painting flat surfaces—pull the brush as shown in Photo 8-19.

Paint *against* the bristles only in certain situations—the lip of siding and shingles, window sashes, door panels, and when cutting out. This involves angling the handle in the direction it is traveling, as shown in Photo 8-20. Wiggle and squish the bristles, especially if the surface is rough or uneven. Remember that painting against the bristles pulls the bristles apart and bends them out of shape, leaving unsightly marks and bumps in the paint. Bent bristles and a disfigured bristle mass cannot hold paint as well, which reduces the brush's ability to hold paint.

*Photo 8-19: Painting with the bristles.*

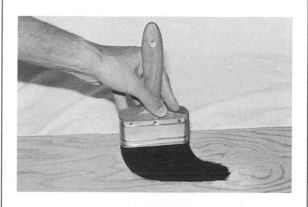

*Photo 8-20: Painting against the bristles.*

Given that wet stain applied over dry stain leaves an ugly lap mark, how do you fix marks left in stain by bugs, ladders, and the occasional palm against the siding? Take a clean paper towel, fold it into quarters, and dip a corner into the stain. Then simply dab the spot with the towel, and let dry. There'll be no lap mark.

You clean up after using oil stain as you do after paint. Use hand cleaner and rags for personal cleanup, and paint thinner for soaking brushes. Clean the paint pots by swirling a little used paint thinner inside them.

Use a stain brush, rather than a standard paintbrush, to apply stain. A stain brush is a wider and stubbier version; its shorter bristles keep the brush from holding too much stain, which controls dripping, and its wider bristle mass compensates for shorter bristles by increasing the area each stroke will cover.

I suggest that you intermix cans of stain, a few gallons at a time, in a 5-gallon mixing bucket. The vehicle and pigment separate easily, so you must be certain to stir stain thoroughly, and the large mixing bucket gives you more room to swirl the stir stick. You have to break up the chunks of pigment that invariably are found on the bottom. Moreover, cans may vary in their concentrations of vehicle and pigment, even when they are from the same producer and the same batch. By combining gallons, you dilute this possible difference, giving the stain a uniform color across the entire job.

Use a 1-gallon paint pot—the 5-inch-wide stain brush cannot fit inside a regular paint bucket's mouth. Transfer stain from the stain bucket to the 5-gallon mixing bucket to the paint pot, then carry the pot with you when staining.

Apply stain systematically, as you would paint—work top to bottom, side to side. Use lots of drop cloths. Because stain is less viscous than paint, it naturally drips.

Apply two coats of stain. A single coat may not produce the color tone you desire and increases the chance for lap marks. A second coat should deepen the color, and it will increase the life span of the stain job. You need wait only 24 hours before applying the second coat of stain.

## CHAPTER 9

# Rolling, Cutting Out, and Spraying

Rolling and spraying are two techniques that really speed up painting. Imagine how long it would take you to paint four living room walls with a brush alone—using a roller saves you many hours and leaves a smoother finish. And think how many Saturdays it might take you to brush paint on porch railings or attic vents (like those on the house shown on the jacket). An inexpensive hand-held spray gun paints intricate pieces like these quickly and easily. In this chapter you'll learn how and when to use rollers and sprayers to your best advantage.

### Using a Roller

Rollers are terrific. They spread finishes quickly, easily, and neatly. You can use them indoors and

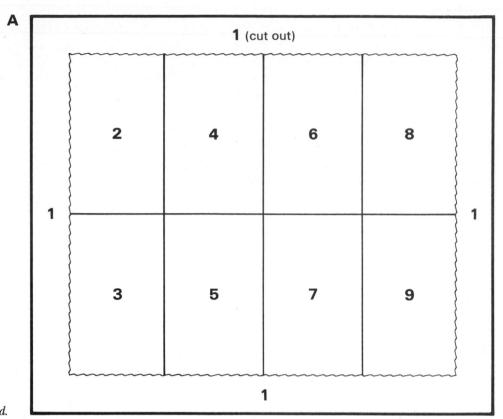

*Illustration 9-1: Rolling a ceiling, wall, or floor with latex (A), or oil paint (B). Sections are numbered in the order that they should be painted.*

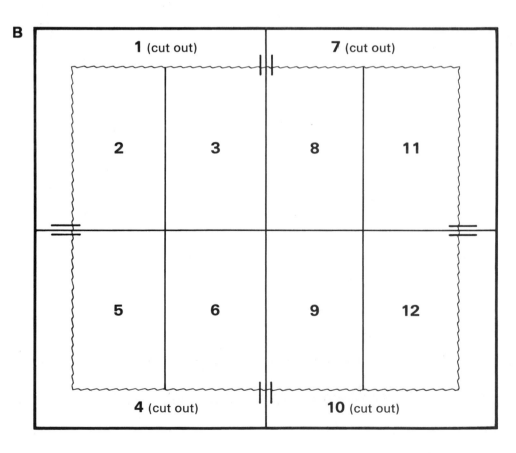

outdoors, on ceilings, walls, and floors, and with both oil and latex paints. As discussed in Chapter 6, you need to match the surface texture to the roller nap—long nap for painting rough surfaces such as brick and cinderblock, medium nap for painting textured surfaces such as drywall, and thin nap for polyurethaning smooth surfaces such as hardwood floors.

Indoor painting goes quickly with a roller. You start from the ceiling and work your way down. Cut out and roll the ceiling, then cut out and roll the walls, then paint the woodwork.

I recommend using latex paint indoors. It dries quickly, doesn't emit annoying or toxic fumes, and leaves no lap marks. You just cut out and roll, cut out and roll, all at your own pace, taking breaks whenever you wish. For example, you can cut out, allow the paint to dry overnight, then roll the following morning.

### Rolling with Oil

You may use oil paint, but it requires a different application technique because it may leave lap marks. This requires you to plan a painting strategy and to work quickly. Although oil paint does not dry as quickly as latex, you are apt to create these shiny marks when you apply paint over any area that has already been done and allowed to dry. This means that you cannot cut out a large room and then leisurely paint the ceiling and walls: the cut-out paint will have dried enough to create lap marks along the corners.

To keep a wet paint edge at all times, cut out only as much of the room as you can roll in 15 minutes. Then roll within that section. Next, cut out a another modest-sized section immediately to the left or right, and roll that. Be certain to feather the roller into the previously painted section, both to keep the edges wet and also to smooth out paint lines. You must continue painting until you either finish that particular ceiling or wall or reach a natural break such as a chair molding.

### Cutting Out

As efficient as a roller is, it can't reach joints between ceiling and walls. The job of painting these joints with a brush is known as cutting out. This strip is then overlapped with the roller.

There are two types of cutting out: I call them rough cutout and fine cutout. A rough cutout is filling the joints with paint as quickly as possible

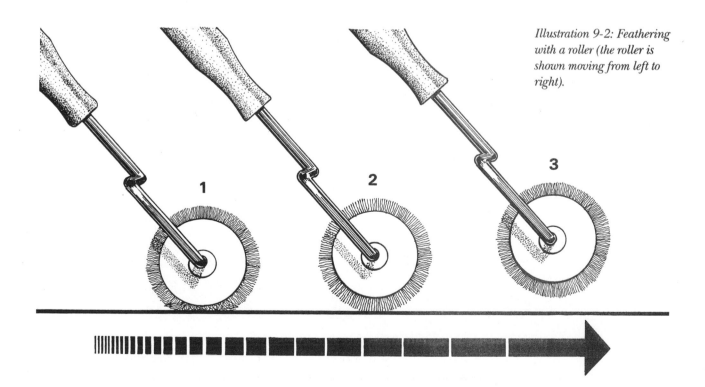

*Illustration 9-2: Feathering with a roller (the roller is shown moving from left to right).*

with no regard for neatness or accuracy; a fine cutout is carefully guiding the brush along the joint so that paint does not overlap onto the other side. Only when there are different colored paints on either side of the joint do you need to fine cutout. To cut out, use a 2½-inch beveled brush.

For rough cutouts, paint an inch or two out onto each surface, so that the roller can get close enough to overlap. Don't try to run a tidy strip, because the roller overlap will cover the rough cutout edge. You can brush either vertically or horizontally.

I find that a doughnut roller makes the rough cutout a lot easier. Just dip the doughnut into the roller pan, and run it up and down along the joint. By attaching an extension pole to the doughnut

*Photo 9-2: This is an example of a rough cutout. The dark clapboard paint overlaps onto the molding. Overlapping the paint like this allows you to paint the clapboard very quickly.*

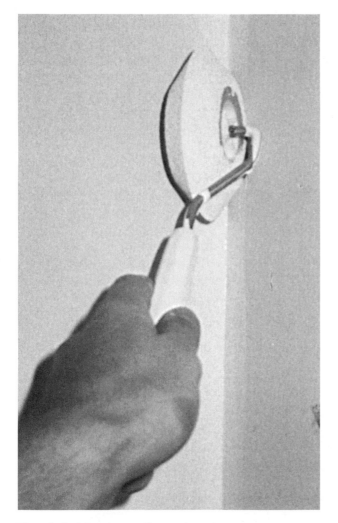

*Photo 9-1: A doughnut roller speeds cutting out.*

*Photo 9-3: This is an example of a fine cutout, which is made by using a 2-inch beveled brush to apply white trim paint to the molding.*

roller, you can cut out with little ladder climbing.

When you're cutting out along trim that will be painted another color or with enamel, you should overlap the wall paint. As shown in Photos 9-2 and 9-3, wall paint that overlaps the trim will be covered by a careful job with the trim paint. So, there is no point in cutting out the wall paint to a razor edge. Moreover, overlapping the dark wall paint onto the trim makes fine cutting out much easier because it creates a smooth surface over which to paint.

When fine cutting out, put only ½ inch of paint on your brush in order to avoid dripping. This requires many more dips into the paint bucket, but will enable your brush to leave a sharper cutout line on the molding because you can control the paint flow.

Be your own worst critic when it comes to fine cutouts. It's a painter's paradox that the smallest areas grab the most attention. This care separates the pretty good job from the superb job.

Getting a straight fine cutout line is much

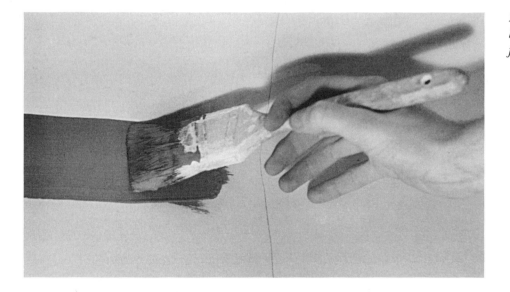

*Photo 9-4: To help steady your hand, try dragging your pinky finger as a guide.*

*Photo 9-5: Masking tape helps to compensate for a less-than-steady painting hand.*

easier if your first pass totally covers the molding edge. If you miss, and have to go back and touch up, this puts extra paint on the molding and increases the chance of drips and an uneven edge.

If you have trouble holding the brush steady, drag your pinky finger along the wall or apply masking tape to the wall when painting either molding or contrasting colors on walls and ceiling. Be aware, however, that paint may creep under the tape despite your best efforts; at other times, some of the new wall paint may come off with the tape. To touch up these spots, make a touch-up brush for very delicate work by cutting 20 or so bristles off a 4-inch brush with a utility knife and taping them together.

## Get Rolling

A roller will perform for you much better if you take the trouble to properly load it with paint. Allow the roller to sink halfway into the paint pool. While spreading paint on the roller by moving it up and down the ramp of the pan, occasionally lift it and let it spin so that the dry areas on the nap do not keep coinciding with those on the pan. Paint should be evenly spread through the nap before rolling.

### Getting Ready to Paint a Room

Take the small furniture out of the room. Large items can be moved to the center of the room, or a minimum of at least 6 feet from the walls. Cover them with a clean drop cloth or, better yet, a new plastic sheet under a heavy drop cloth. You need to take everything off the walls, of course, including picture nails and outlet plates. Wall cracks and holes should be spackled and sanded smooth. Clean cobwebs out of the corners. Use masking tape to protect hinges, doorknobs, mirrors, built-ins, and tile. Lay drop cloths to cover all of the floor.

Arrange lamps to provide plenty of light. For makeshift work lights, wrap foil reflectors around the shade harp of the table lamps, and use 100-watt bulbs if the lamps are rated to take them.

### The Ceiling

When painting a room, the ceiling comes first, then the walls, and finally the woodwork. Cut out the entire ceiling, then roll it. To make things

*Photo 9-6: You can make work lights simply by placing foil reflectors behind the bulbs of old table lamps.*

easier, try these ideas. First, rough cut out the ceiling perimeter so that the paint extends into the ceiling about 2 inches and overlaps about 1 inch down on the wall. By making sure that paint is fully covering the ceiling-to-wall joint, you'll make fine cutting out on the wall much easier. Second, when you're ready to roll, your first roller stroke can be along this rough cutout line (instead of beginning right away with the W stroke). This extends the cutout farther into the ceiling so that later on you can feather the roller into the ceiling-to-wall joint without slamming into the wall. Roll carefully along the cutout line so that you don't scrape the roller end on the wall.

Roll the rest of the ceiling. Rolling a W on the ceiling is sometimes awkward, because you have to work with an extension pole (so if it's easier for you, roll on the paint in straight lines). Leave small spaces between strokes, then double back to smooth out the paint.

The final strokes should all be in one direction and feathered into all previously rolled paint.

### The Walls

Before cutting out the walls, allow the ceiling paint to dry (30 minutes to 2 hours for latex, 2 to 24 hours for oil). Once the ceiling-to-wall joint is dry,

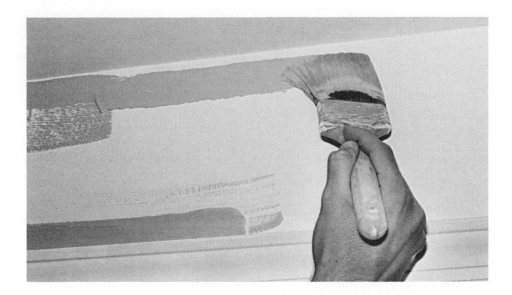

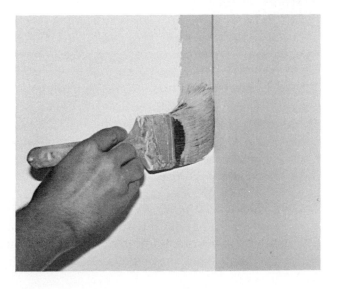

*Photos 9-7, 9-8, and 9-9: Cut out the top of the wall at the ceiling (the top and middle photos), then move on to the joint between walls (bottom photo), and then to the bottom of the wall at the baseboard.*

you can start with the walls. If you are applying the same paint on the walls, you'll notice that the ceiling-to-wall joint is already cut out from your work on the ceiling. Now just rough cut out the wall-to-wall joints, run the roller along the ceiling-to-wall cutout line to extend it farther into the wall, and begin rolling Ws.

If you are applying a different color paint to the walls, you must fine cut out the ceiling-to-wall joint with the wall paint. To paint a crisp edge along the ceiling, I find it easiest if I first lay a thick strip of paint along the wall just ½ inch below the ceiling joint (Photo 9-7), then carefully draw the brush against the bristles for a second pass to bring the paint to that joint. Next, I pull the brush back along the wall to smooth and spread the paint (Photo 9-8). If this doesn't work for you, try the reverse: Draw the brush along the ceiling-to-wall joint (against the bristles), then extend this cutout line with a broader second stroke. Finally, I cut out the wall-to-wall joints (Photo 9-9) and above the baseboards, and I'm ready to roll the walls.

The best way to cover a wall quickly and evenly is by rolling "Ws." Note that the first W spreads a lot of paint over a large area, leaving V gaps. If you were to cover all of an area at once, the paint would be too thick where you first placed the roller on the wall, because progressively less paint is laid down as you move outward.

Work from top to bottom, starting at an upper corner. Next, backtrack over the Ws (as seen in Illustration 9-3) to smooth out the thick paint. The finish strokes, in the last illustration, serve to smooth out the paint lines. Run the roller vertically, bottom to top. As the roller nears the end of the block, feather the paint by slowly pulling the still-spinning roller off the surface.

Repeat these steps to cover the wall with paint, feathering each W in turn for a smooth job. After allowing the wall paint to dry, use a brush to paint the woodwork, windows, doors, baseboards, ceiling, and chair moldings.

### More than One Color

A multitone paint scheme can really jazz up a room. But it is somewhat more complicated to apply. You must be certain to let the first color dry before beginning to apply the second color. For example, if the ceiling is white and the walls are blue, paint the ceiling and let it dry. Then paint the walls. After the walls dry, paint the woodwork. This prevents you from mixing wet blue paint with white and getting a rainbow of dark and pale blues.

Because latex dries quickly, you can paint any room using any color combination without waiting for hours on end; because oil dries slowly, however, you may need to wait as long as 24 hours before being able to continue painting walls or woodwork without risking paint rainbows.

## Spray Equipment

There are two kinds of sprayers used for painting houses. Compressors are large cylindrical tanks, pressurized by electric motors, which force paint through a long hose and out a spray nozzle. They are widely used by professionals because they are fast, durable, and adaptable for different kinds of jobs. But they are expensive and cumbersome. What's more, compressor sprayers generate a lot of stray mist, and they should be used with a respirator for lung protection.

Small, self-contained hand-held sprayers are a better choice for most homeowners. They are lightweight, easy to handle, and inexpensive, costing roughly $100 plus attachments (they may also be rented at equipment shops). Because they produce little stray mist, these sprayers don't require you to wear a respirator, and they can be used indoors. There are a few disadvantages to hand-held sprayers, however. They aren't as quick or as versatile as compressors; they tend to be fragile, with a number of plastic parts that wear out with use; they have a tendency to accumulate paint near the spray outlet, which causes paint spitting; and their 1-quart paint capacity means frequent refills. Nonetheless, these sprayers produce excellent results and save you lots of time.

A sprayer's greatest value is in painting tricky surfaces, such as shutters, louvered doors, wicker furniture, picket fences, and fancy molding along the roofline of the house. It should be mentioned that there is some controversy in the painting profession over whether sprayed paint is as durable as brushed paint. My experience has been that, if

*Illustration 9-3: By rolling large W's over the wall, you spread the paint more evenly.*

applied properly, sprayed paint will last as long as brushed paint.

### Spraying Siding

If you have never used a sprayer before, get the feel of it by practicing on scrap wood or newspaper taped to a wall.

Before getting down to work, remove outlet plates, thermometers, plant holders, and all other hardware that would be damaged by paint spray. Apply masking tape to vents, hose faucets, and other immovable hardware. Cover masonry and bushes with drop cloths.

Hold the sprayer with two hands at all times: one hand grabs the sprayer handle and pulls the trigger, and the other hand supports the paint cup. The paint cup clips have a tendency to come undone, dumping paint on your shoes.

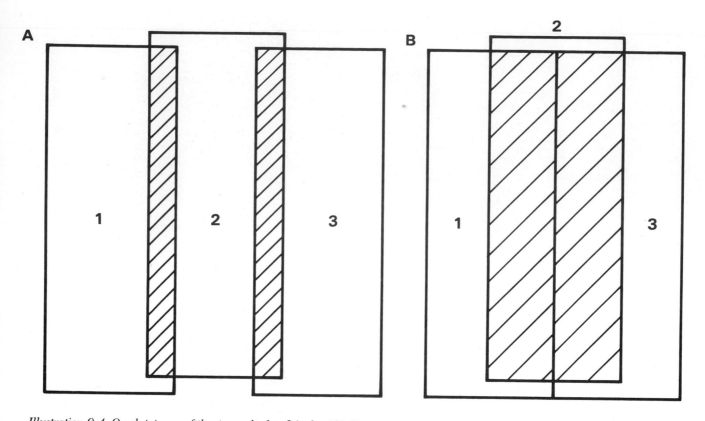

*Illustration 9-4: Overlap passes of the sprayer by 1 to 2 inches (A). For greater coverage, overlap as shown in B.*

With the sprayer at head level, pull the trigger and start moving the gun downward until it is level with your waist; then *slowly* bend at the knees and ease into a squatting position, continuing to hold the sprayer level with your waist. This technique enables you to spray continuously down the siding. Squat as far as you can without getting uncomfortable, and release the trigger just before you stop. Stand up and make another vertical pass to one side of the first.

Allow the spray to overlap onto trim boards to guarantee that paint covers the surface all the way to its edge. And overlap each pass of the sprayer by 1 or 2 inches to ensure that you don't leave vertical strips of unpainted siding.

The spray should hit the surface at a slightly upward angle. Tipping the sprayer back so the spray shoots upward a bit ensures that the siding lips will be painted.

Do not tip the sprayer forward. Paint will spill out of the spray gate opening.

Move the sprayer at a constant speed at all times. Generally, 3 to 4 inches per second is a good pace for even paint coverage. Uneven downward speed will result in uneven paint application: some parts of the siding may get so much paint that sags develop; other siding areas may not be fully covered and show bare spots.

Keep the sprayer a constant distance from the siding. I find about 8 inches is best; this keeps the paint flow as thick as possible while at the same time prevents sagging.

If the trim boards and siding are to be the same type and color of paint, be sure to angle the spray so that their joints are fully covered with paint. Keep a 2½-inch beveled brush nearby to smooth out spits and sags; these may be caused by holding the sprayer too close to the surface or by moving it too slowly.

Once you start painting with a sprayer, try not to let it stand unused for more than 30 minutes. Otherwise, the paint will begin to harden, which ruins the plastic parts. To minimize the number of breaks you have to take, organize your spraying sequence. Get everything ready to be painted, apply masking tape, lay drop cloths, and so on. Then fill the sprayer with paint, spray, and promptly clean all paint out of the unit. Manufacturers' recommendations for cleaning their sprayers do vary. But it is essential to clean the sprayer completely after each use. You should immerse all plastic parts in clear paint thinner, if you're using oil paint, or very warm water, if you're using latex. A gallon bucket with at least a quart of liquid will do. Rub off all paint accumulations with your fingers as soon as possible. Once the major chunks of paint are removed from the plastic pieces, scrub out remaining paint deposits with a hard-bristled toothbrush. Clean all parts as thoroughly as possible; be sure to get even the smallest bits of paint out of cracks and joints. Finally, dry off each plastic part with clean paper towels or rags. Thorough cleaning will help your sprayer last for years.

*Photo 9-10: Remove lamps and lanterns to be sprayed, after shutting off power to them at the breaker or fuse box.*

## Spraying from a Can

The most likely candidates for spraying with a can of paint are iron railings and exterior lanterns. Iron railings take forever to paint with a brush, but hardly any time with a spray can. Wire brush the rust off the railing, place masking tape around the concrete where the railing post meets the walkway, lay a drop cloth under the railing, and spray. Work systematically. Paint the undersides first, then the sides, then the top. Or vice versa. This ensures that you do not miss any spots.

Lanterns should be removed from the house before spraying; do so only after turning off the power at the breaker or fuse box. Pop out the glass, take off the rust with a wire brush, lay the fixture on newspaper, and spray with rust-inhibitive paint.

Spray only in calm weather, and keep an extra can of spray paint on hand to ensure you don't run out with only a few feet left. Don't bother painting gutters and downspouts with rust-inhibitive paint, unless they are bare metal and require a metal primer. I've found that ordinary house paint adheres very well to metal surfaces as long as peeling paint has been scraped off. Remember that you can hide the marks of dry, spilled paint on roofs and driveways by spraying with flat black or grey paint.

# CHAPTER 10

# Trim, Shutters, Windows, and Doors

This chapter gives tips on painting trim boards, shutters, windows, doors, gutters, and steps. The following sections explain only the brush movements peculiar to each of these pieces.

## Trim Boards and Window Trim

You have to make a few decisions before painting trim. First, is the trim going to be the same color as the siding? If it will be, you can save time by painting the siding and trim all at once. When you are atop the plank, paint everything within reach—siding, trim boards, and window trim. In this way, you need to circle the house only once with your plank and ladders to paint the entire exterior.

If the trim will be a different color, paint the siding and let it dry before painting the trim boards, window trim, doors, and so on. This means that you will have to circle your house twice, resetting ladders and plank. This, of course, takes more time, but it ensures that you will avoid the rainbow effect of mixing different colored wet paints. You also are spared the inconvenience of dealing with two paint buckets and two brushes at one time, which can be cumbersome on the plank.

A second consideration when painting a two-tone color scheme is whether the trim sides should be painted the siding color or the trim color. Photo

*Photo 10-1: You have to decide whether to paint the trim side the color of the siding or the color of the trim face.*

10-1 shows the side of the window trim painted with white trim paint. In terms of surface area, trim sides seem like a trivial matter—but in terms of painting time, they are a huge consideration. Painting trim sides is tedious and arduous because you must fine cut out along each of the clapboards, and the sharper appearance is usually not worth the effort.

Generally, you should paint the sides the trim color if the trim is in a very conspicuous place, such as on a porch or near an entryway.

It stands to reason that the trim side facing a window should be painted the trim color (Photo 10-2). Take care to avoid getting paint on aluminum storm windows—a mark of a careless amateur.

Do you need to use a special paint for trim? No. You can use any paint you like—oil or latex, flat or semi-gloss. And you aren't locked in by your choice of siding paint. It's perfectly fine to apply latex on the trim when you've used oil on the siding, and vice versa. Simply buy the best exterior paint you can find.

Having said this, I would suggest you make things easy for yourself by using either oil-based paint or latex paint for everything. You then won't have to bother with different drying times and with recalling if a particular brush should soak in paint thinner or be rinsed in water.

What color should you paint the trim? Your first reaction might be to pick up dozens of color swatches from the paint store, but a better way is to look at color schemes in your area. You may really like the way cream-colored siding and black shutters look on a house across town. If so, great! Knock on the front door, tell them you think they have terrific taste, and ask which paint brand and custom colors they used.

How long does it take to paint trim? As a rough guide, plan on spending 1 hour to paint three window frames, or 30 feet of trim board, or 20 feet of finely cutout ceiling molding. Refer to Chapter 1 for more information on estimating time. Generally speaking, your time will be split 70–30 between painting the siding and trim, respectively, if both are the same color and type of paint. But if siding and trim are painted with different colors or types of paint, count on them taking roughly equal amounts of time.

Think of "trim" as any interior or exterior

*Photo 10-2: Trim sides that face windows should be painted with trim paint.*

board that surrounds a window or door or runs vertically or horizontally along the side or length of the house. All trim is painted the exact same way: first its sides, and then its face.

### Trim Sides

If you have decided to take the time to paint the sides of trim pieces as well as the faces, there are two methods. First, you can apply 1½-inch masking tape on the siding flush with the trim edge (the siding should already be painted and dry). Paint the trim side, then remove the tape immediately.

The second technique requires you to have a steady hand and an especially good 2½-inch beveled brush. No masking tape is used—you simply pull the brush along the trim side, going against the bristles for best results. Keep a gap of ⅛ inch

or so between the bristle tips and the siding to make sure trim paint doesn't run down the newly painted walls.

If your house has shutters, then they will conceal the trim sides. In this case, definitely do not paint the trim sides—you'll never see them.

### Trim Board Faces

Remember that the siding's final coat of paint must be dry before the final coat of a different colored trim paint is applied. First, apply the paint *across the wood grain,* in order to ensure that all of the board is covered with plenty of paint. (In time you may be able to get good coverage with the standard with-the-grain brush stroke.) Start from the edge opposite the siding, and lift the brush off the trim board before it reaches the end. This prevents the bristles from slapping against the freshly painted siding.

Smooth out the paint by brushing *with* the wood grain. If your brush is too large to pull down the trim board without overhanging and getting paint on the siding, you can turn the brush diagonal to the trim board to reduce its effective width.

Use brand new brushes for cutting out. The newer the brush, the better the cutout line. Once a brush has been soaked in thinner and spun a few times, it loses its ability to cut a really straight line and to hold and smooth paint. Aging brushes also tend to have errant bristles that stick out from the bristle mass and leave small hairline streaks of trim paint on the siding; you can extend the life of an aging brush by cutting off these bristles at the metal band with a razor.

Brushes lose their effectiveness quickly when drawn against the bristles. To straighten the bristles, drag the brush against the inner rim of the paint bucket a few times.

Use clean paper towels instead of cloth rags to wipe paint off storm window housings. Cloth rags clog quickly, which then causes you only to smear paint over the housing instead of removing it. If you are not painting the window sash, keep storm windows closed to protect the sash and panes from siding paint. If you are painting the sash, remove the storm windows and paint the window trim and the sash at the same time.

Use the plank to paint trim whenever possible, especially if you are painting a large bay window or

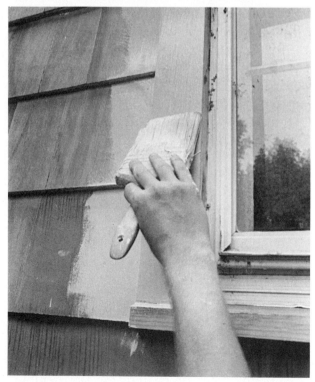

*Photos 10-3 and 10-4: Apply paint to trim faces in two steps: against the grain (photo above) and then with the grain (photo below).*

a second-floor eave. I've found that the ladder alone is best only when painting vertical trim boards on the house corners.

## Roof Trim

Peak roof trim can be difficult and dangerous to paint because it is so high off the ground. Before you even think of attempting to reach roof trim, evaluate your own physical strength, tolerance of heights, balance, and in very real terms, nerve.

You have three options when confronted with lofty roof trim. The best is getting some nimble neighborhood kid to do it for you. This may be a job for someone else if you are not comfortable doing it yourself.

The second option is to do it yourself from a long extension ladder. Climbing up a tall ladder is risky, however.

The least desirable option is to climb on the roof and reach over the edge to paint the trim. If done properly and carefully, it is a useful technique. But it is a dangerous maneuver because you could lose your hand grip or footing and fall off the edge. Remember that I mention this only as a last resort. People die of falls from these heights, and I certainly cannot tell from my desk how to tailor these methods for you. Only you can determine if this technique is suitable, given your abilities and disposition.

With that warning having been said, here are two variations on painting trim from the roof. First, you can do it lying down. I prefer this position, because it keeps your center of gravity as low as possible and lets you see what you are doing. You lie on your stomach at the top of the roof, as flat as possible and with your feet lower than your head. Hang the paint bucket off the side of the roof by sticking the pothook's sharp point into the roof shingles. Spread your legs to give your feet better traction on the roof. Hold the paintbrush in your outside hand. Stick your head out over the roof edge until you can see the roof trim directly beneath your head, grabbing on to the overhanging roof shingles with your inside arm to steady you and keep you from sliding down the roof. Paint the roof trim within your outside arm's reach, moving top to bottom. Do not overextend yourself: when you cannot comfortably reach any more roof trim, move down the roof in the following way.

Put the brush in the bucket. Lift the bucket by the pothook and secure it a few feet down the roof edge so that it hangs just below your waist. Now, with your hands completely free, grab the roof edge with your outside hand; your inside palm rests flat on the roof shingles. Do a push-up to raise yourself just off the roof, and inch downwards on your palms and toes until your head reaches the hanging bucket. Then resume painting.

Stop painting when your feet come within 3 feet of the gutter—you cannot safely paint this lower section of the roof trim from the roof because you need some distance between you and the gutter in order to catch yourself if you start sliding. Use a ladder to reach these lower ends of the roof trim.

The second technique is accomplished sitting down. Sit near the edge of the roof, your feet anchoring you as shown in Photo 10-5, and paint the trim "blind." You have to paint by feel, because you can't safely lean far enough over to see clearly where the brush contacts the surface. But you can feel the roof trim through the brush well enough that you can paint fairly accurately. Stop painting when your feet come within 3 feet of the gutter. You should always have a stretch of roof on which to catch yourself, should you start sliding. As with the first technique, use a ladder to finish the job.

## Safety Up on the Roof

Wear long pants and a shirt to protect your skin from hot, abrasive roof shingles. You'll be scooting around on your seat and upper thighs, and if you wear shorts your backside will get very scratched and raw.

Wear sneakers that have soles which grip exceptionally well. When you walk along asphalt roof shingles, your feet tear small pebbles out of the tar

*Photo 10-5: If you feel steady enough, you can reach over the edge of the roof to paint roof trim.*

*Photo 10-6: The ladder should extend far enough above the roof to afford a grip for the hands when climbing on and off.*

matting. These small pebbles act like the marbles in old-time movies that cause the bad guys to fall down during the big chase. If your soles cannot overcome the ball-bearing effect of the pebbles, you won't be able to stop yourself if you begin sliding down the roof.

Be very careful and alert when walking and sitting on the roof. Walk with sea legs (a slight bend in your knees), moving slowly and thoughtfully. Lean uphill, with your weight toward the top of the roof; if you slip or fall, you will tend to fall upward, not downward. And do not walk close to the gutter. If you get within 5 feet of it, one misstep would place your next get-my-balance-back step in thin air.

You shouldn't carry a full bucket of paint around on a roof, to minimize the damage if you happened to drop it. I suggest putting just one quart in a gallon bucket. Carry the bucket and brush in the same hand, with the brush handle pinched between two fingers and hanging in the bucket. This leaves you with a free hand, which makes it easier to keep your balance.

The steepness of a roof is known as its pitch. If the pitch of the roof is unusually steep, use a metal ridge jack to secure a ladder to the roof (see Chapter 7) or nail a makeshift ladder into the roof, if the roof is asphalt. This ladder can be as simple as strips of wood nailed to the roof itself or nailed to a wooden plank that is nailed to the roof. After removing the ladder, remember to fill in the nail holes with roofing tar (available in tubes for use in a caulking gun); then hammer a large-headed roofing nail into the filled holes, and cover the nail head with more roofing tar.

As a final safety tip, climb on and off the roof at the lowest possible point. This ensures that the extension ladder will be at its sturdiest. Be sure to extend the ladder two or three rungs above the gutter line so that you have something to grab on to with your hands.

## Painting Shutters

At this point in your painting project, the prepped shutters should be waiting in the garage to be painted. Remember that shutters are the

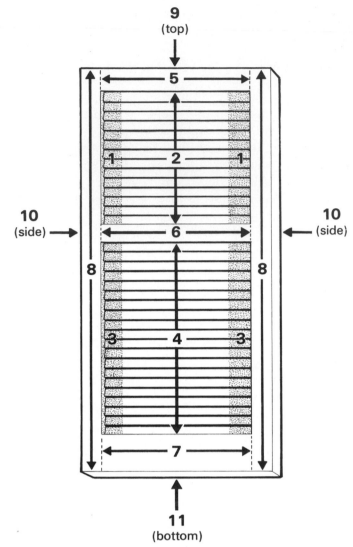

*Illustration 10-1: This is the sequence for painting shutters with a brush. Paint the bottom (11) only after the shutter is re-installed.*

buffer in your work schedule, because they can be painted on rainy days and in the evening hours when other work comes to a halt.

Shutters can be done most easily with a hand-held sprayer. A sprayer is far more expensive than a brush, of course, but it cuts the time required by 80 to 90 percent. A shutter takes a skilled painter 30 minutes with a brush, whereas with a sprayer, the job can be done in just 2 or 3 minutes. If you've got 20 shutters, that's a savings of 9 hours.

## Painting Shutters with a Brush

If you only have a few pairs of shutters to paint, you'll probably choose to do them with a brush rather than buy a sprayer.

Sweep out the garage before painting or stacking shutters there. Dust sticks to paint like crazy and can ruin the job. Lay a drop cloth on the floor and rest a shutter flat on two sawhorses or garbage cans without the lids. You can also lay shutters on an extension ladder covered with a drop cloth.

Use a 4-inch brush—it may feel a bit awkward, but with practice, you'll be able to paint twice as fast as with a 2½-inch brush. Begin by painting all joints where the louvers meet the frame. Stick the bristle tips into the corners and draw the brush just an inch or so out into the louver. Use plenty of paint to be sure that you cover all of the joint. Next, paint the louvers by sticking the bristle tips into the joint at one end of the louvers and pulling the brush to the corner at the other end. For best coverage, brush in the reverse direction as well, and feather the brush so that you leave no brush marks in the paint.

Once the louvers are painted, move to the top and sides of the frame. The first brush stroke should be *against* the wood grain. Then, smooth the paint by brushing with the grain. Watch for drips down the face of the shutter. Do not paint the bottom now, because you'll be stacking the shutter to dry; instead, wait until the shutter has dried, either before or after installation, before painting the bottoms.

Don't waste your time painting the backsides of shutters. There's no reason to make unnecessary work by prepping and painting something no one will ever see. The only prep and painting work you should do on the backsides of shutters is quick-and-dirty scraping and spot priming to seal bare wood from weather.

To carry a freshly painted shutter to its drying place, lift it by slipping two screwdrivers under a louver. Be careful—you can crack the louver if your movements are not smooth.

Check drying shutters for drips and sags 10 minutes after painting. The joints between louvers and frame are prime locations for dripping paint. Use a brush to smooth out dips and sags.

To stack a large number of drying shutters in the garage, start by placing two shutters perpendicular to each other, and lean them together so that they support themselves. The shutters should touch

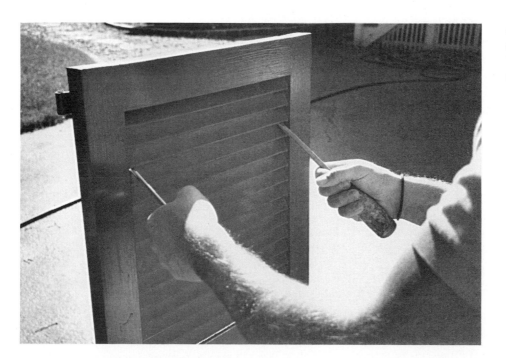

*Photo 10-7: How can you carry a freshly painted shutter? With two sturdy screwdrivers inserted under a sturdy louver.*

*Photo 10-8: Stack wet shutters like a house of cards.*

each other on their sides at only one point. (Picture the way you would stack two playing cards in forming the walls of a card house.) Then lean other shutters, working out from the first couple to form a chain as shown in Photo 10-8.

## Painting Shutters with a Sprayer

First, find a partner if possible. Spraying moves extra fast if a helper is on hand to position shutters to be sprayed, stack them to dry, smooth out drips, and so on.

Protect the surrounding area from paint spray by laying a heavy drop cloth on the ground. To support the shutters, place the plank or an extension ladder on top of two sawhorses or garbage cans. Drape a second drop cloth over the plank or ladder.

Be sure to have a scraper on hand to catch any peeling that may have escaped your notice. Lean the shutters against the covered plank or ladder, and support them from below on cinderblocks or scrap wood so that you can spray the lowest louvers without soaking the drop cloth with paint.

Spray the shutter, beginning with the right louver-to-frame joints. Work from the top down. Angle the sprayer upward so that the paint reaches into the joints; notice that the painter in Photo 10-9 stands at an angle to the shutter in order to better

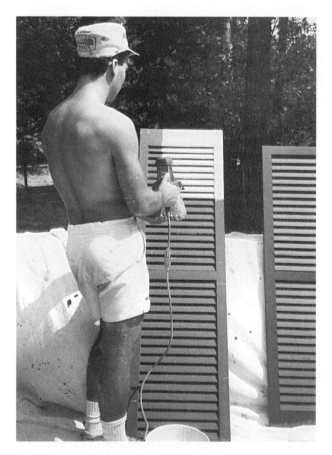

*Photo 10-9: Spray shutters at an angle for best coverage where the louvers meet the frame. Paint one side of the shutter, working top to bottom, then move to the other side.*

direct paint spray into the joints. If the paint was sprayed perpendicular to the shutter, coverage would be poor in the joints.

Continue spraying to the bottom of the shutter —you should be able to cover the entire right side, including the frame, in a single downward stroke. Adjust your downward speed or the sprayer's opening so that the paint fully covers the shutter's original color.

Next, do the left side of the shutter in the same manner. You should be able to cover the entire face of the shutter with just these two downward strokes of the sprayer.

To spray the sides of the frame, adjust the spray length to just 2 inches. Then draw the sprayer top to bottom along both left and right sides. Paint the top of the shutter with a brush. The bottom of the shutter should be painted after the rest of the shutter has dried. Stack the shutters to dry as explained for painting shutters with a brush, above (Photo 10-8).

## Painting Windows

I'll tell you how to paint a double-hung window, with its two movable sashes, because it is a more complex job than painting hinged awning and casement windows. The information here should cover everything you need to know to paint these hinged windows as well.

To avoid the most frequent gaffe made by the novice painter—painting the windows shut—lift the lower sash and pull down the upper sash. You may have to slap your palm against the sash frames (not the small, delicate wooden muntins that hold the individual panes of glass in place) in order to get them to move. You can also loosen up frozen windows by running a utility knife into the joint between the sash and its track.

Now look at the window. You'll see a piece of wood that had been hidden—the bottom frame member of the upper sash. If the previous painters were sloppy, it's very likely that this board has lots of drips, or no paint at all. Scrape away any loose paint and drips from this board, and paint as much of the exposed lower half of the upper sash as you can reach.

Next, paint the window trench—the slot into which the lower sash slides when fully closed.

*Photo 10-10: Reverse upper and lower sashes so that you can paint the lower frame member of the upper sash.*

Then turn your attention to the vertical tracks that carry the sash. Older windows have wooden tracks that likely already have paint on them. Each paint job adds a layer to the tracks, and in time this buildup may prevent sashes from sliding at all. So, paint window tracks only if they are peeling. New windows have aluminum tracks, which should never be painted.

Push the upper sash back up and pull the lower sash back down, so that they are in their normal positions, but leave gaps of 3 inches or so at top and bottom. These two gaps keep air flowing between the sashes and the frame, preventing the sashes from freezing up in their tracks.

Finish painting the upper sash, and do all of the lower sash. Next, paint the molding around the window itself.

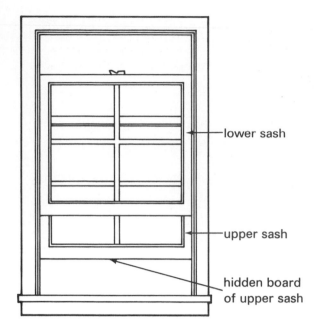

*Illustration 10-2: Reverse sashes to paint all of a window's parts.*

— lower sash

— upper sash

hidden board
of upper sash

I use about ½ inch of paint on a 2½- or 4-inch brush. Paint with the brush held as shown in Photo 10-11. Press the bristle tips into the one corner, and pull the brush across to the next corner.

Next, paint the face of the muntins—the thin wood strips between panes in a divided-lite sash. Then paint the sashes, including the piece that will be concealed when they are returned to their normal positions. Put about ½ inch of paint on the bristles, brush against the wood grain to cover the wood with paint, then brush with the wood grain to smooth the paint.

Let the window dry 48 to 72 hours. Scrape the paint off the glass when dry; this involves a wait of 2 to 3 days for latex paint, and as long as a week for oil. While you wait, you can re-install screens once the paint is dry to the touch (8 hours for latex, and 24 hours for oil), and remember to slap the sash

Painting the *outside* of a window is the same, except for the altitude and the glazing compound. New glazing compound may still be soft when you are ready to paint. It's best to postpone painting for a week or two until the stuff forms an outer crust hard enough to withstand the force of the brush and subsequent scraping. If you paint over soft compound, you cut off exposure to air and slow the crusting.

People usually dread painting windows because it's such a chore to keep paint off the glass. It takes a steady hand and the patience of a saint to neatly draw paint along the sash. And the task seems monumental when you consider that an average-sized double-hung window with 18 panes has nearly 500 inches of sash to paint.

Some people put masking tape on the glass to avoid getting paint on it. But this takes lots of time, and paint usually seeps under the tape and onto the glass anyway. My solution is to paint the sash as quickly as possible with no regard to paint that lands on the glass; after the paint dries, I scrape the paint off the glass with a razor. As inefficient as this may seem, it's actually the fastest way to paint the sash. The result is also much more thorough and neat.

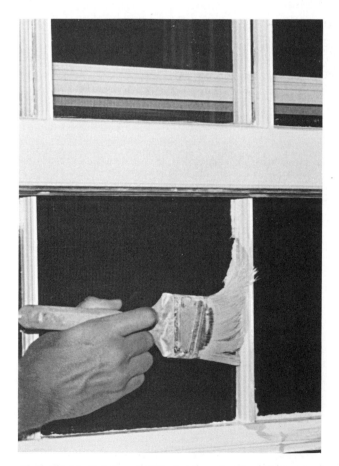

*Photo 10-11: Paint against the bristles—that is, with the bristles bent back.*

*Photo 10-12: Don't overlook the part of the upper sash that will be concealed when the window is in its normal position.*

*Photo 10-13: Wait until the paint has dried on the panes before scraping it.*

frame with your palm to crack the paint seal that would prevent the sashes from sliding. Finally, replace the hardware.

After the paint has thoroughly dried, scrape the paint off the glass with a razor blade and holder sold for that purpose at hardware and paint stores. Put the razor flush against the glass, then push the razor into the sash with short, quick, choppy motions. Use a good deal of force—don't be timid. The glass won't scratch. If the paint is dry enough, it should curl nicely off the glass. Otherwise, it may stick to the razor and smear on the glass; allow the paint to dry completely before scraping.

To slice off the hanging paint shavings, press a corner of the razor into the sash and drag the razor along the joint. Brush away the paint shavings.

It should take you no longer than 45 seconds to scrape the pane of glass in the photos. Scraping is fast work. When scraping the outside of a window, make certain the glazing compound has formed a crust; otherwise, it may be damaged by the razor. Even once the compound is hardened, you should stop the razor $1/16$ inch short of reaching new compound.

You can leave the job here, or do the following to remove that last bit of paint. This painstaking approach takes a long time, and should be used if you have reglazed only a few pieces of sash. Gently push the razor under the remaining paint strip until you just feel the razor sink $1/16$ inch or so under the outer edge of the glazing. Then slowly pull the razor out. To cut off the paint strip, hold the razor perpendicular to the pane of glass at the outer edge of the glazing compound, and push. Drag the razor away from the glazing to pare off the paint. Notice that this process pinches the glazing compound against the glass, forming a good seal.

Change razor blades often. A sharp edge really speeds up scraping. I suggest changing blades after every two panes, or even sooner if they begin to loose their bite. Keep a plastic bucket handy to hold used razor blades, and wear goggles—blades occasionally snap.

To change razor blades, pinch the blade hard with your fingertips at the blade's sharp edge, and pull the razor blade out of the holder. Then take the cardboard wrapping off the new razor, pinch it hard at the tip of its sharp edge, and slide it into the razor holder. By pinching the blade between your fingers, you keep the razor's edge straight up and down between your fingers. This prevents the edge from tipping to one side and cutting you.

## Storm Windows

Storm windows are either metal (usually aluminum) units screwed directly to the window's trim, or wooden frames hanging from the house. In order to paint exterior window sash, you must either slide the two glass sections out of the metal track or remove the wooden framed storm window.

You remove metal storms from *inside* the house: pinch the two side clips to pull the bottom of one glass section toward you so that it pops out of the track. Tip the glass to the left or right to cause one of the upper pins to fall out of its track. You now can pull out the panel completely. Do this to remove both the upper glass section and the screen as well. I suggest that you rest the storms and the screen directly under their window in the order they came out to avoid problems with mismatched pieces

*Photo 10-14: Drag the razor's edge down the pane to remove paint shavings.*

later on. To remove wooden storms, you have to work *outside* from a ladder: lean a ladder up against the house, lift the frame off its hanging hinges, and label its location.

If you are painting only the siding (the window sash may not need painting because the storms give them protection), leave the storms in place to keep siding paint from splattering on the sash. If you get paint drops on the storm window glass, simply let them dry and zip them off with a razor blade.

If you will be painting the window sash, paint the trim boards and the sash at the same time. For example, remove the storms, paint the siding blue, then let dry. Then paint the trim boards and window sashes white. This strategy enables you to speed through the siding painting with just one color and one brush to juggle when atop the plank. Then, you can efficiently go about painting the windows and trim a second color. And, you are spared the risk of mixing colors when applying two paints simultaneously.

Another strategy is to postpone painting the windows for less-than-dry (but not rainy) days when you cannot paint the siding. If yesterday's rain hasn't dried off the siding, you can keep your painting schedule on track by working on windows that were behind the storms. (Paint manufacturers go so far as to say that latex paint can be safely applied over wet surfaces, without risking peeling, because the underlying water must evaporate completely before the paint will dry, but I wouldn't chance it.)

Keep the storms closed until just before you are ready to paint the windows. Check first to make sure the sash is not damp from rain or dew. Once the windows are painted, re-install the storms to protect the windows from siding paint.

## Painting Doors

Garage doors, front doors, bedroom doors, cabinet doors—all are painted the same way. The door should be properly prepped: sand glossy paint lightly by hand with 80- or 50-grit sandpaper, brush paint dust away, and see that all peeling paint is scraped and sanded off. Here is a sequence of painting steps for best results.

First, wrap masking tape around doorknobs, hinges, and other hardware not easily removed. Remove metal doorknob plates, air brakes, door knockers, and doorbell buttons. Place a drop cloth under the door.

Use a 2½-inch brush, at least to start. With

*Photo 10-15: Quickly dry brush the shavings off the glass.*

experience, you'll find that a 4-inch brush paints twice as fast and can be used nimbly; if you need to get into tight corners with it, simply turn it sideways so only a portion of the bristle mass touches the surface.

Paint the door in the sequence shown in Illustration 10-3. Start with the top panels (number 1). Paint their moldings and borders against the bristles. Then paint the panels themselves by brushing in several directions to spread the paint; smooth by brushing with the wood grain.

Next paint the frame boards between the panels. Apply the paint *across* the wood grain, and then smooth the paint *with* the grain. This step takes some care, but is important because paint that runs against the wood grain will create a messy, checker-board effect. Illustration 10-3 indicates the direction of the grain of a typical door's components. The trick is to change brush stroke direction where boards meet at right angles, as boards 8 and 5 do. To make a sharp edge where they meet, place the bristles flat on the very end of board 5 and draw the brush away from board 8, toward the center of the board. You can do this *after* board 8 has been painted, because the paint on board 5 will still be wet.

The door edges can be painted the color of either face. Just be sure to be consistent: an edge should be one color, not two. Finally, do everything that surrounds the door itself—moldings, lintel, jamb, and threshold.

Check for paint drips after 10 minutes. Paint often accumulates in the panel corners and begins to drip down the frame boards. Smooth away drips with your brush. Keep the drop cloth under the drying door for at least an hour. Finish up by removing masking tape and replacing hardware.

You can efficiently spray doors if you will be painting many the same color. But don't bother if you have only a few to paint, because of the time required to set up the spraying system and getting the doors outside. Hammer the pins out of the hinges, label the door's location, and place the door on an outdoor plank-and-drop-cloth system as described for shutters above. (Of course you'll spray garage doors right where they are.) Aim the sprayer as directed in the shutter section.

## Painting Everything Else

The following tips should be followed only after you are familiar with the painting basics described so far in this book. Outlined here are techniques for painting baseboards, railings, gutters and downspouts, and steps.

### Baseboards

Baseboards must be painted with extra care when they run along fine wood floors or carpeting. On bare floors, lay 1½-inch masking tape on the floor, flush with the baseboard. Overlap the tape onto the baseboard about 1/16 inch; otherwise, paint will seep under the tape and leave marks on the floor. Be sure that the tape seals tightly. A drop

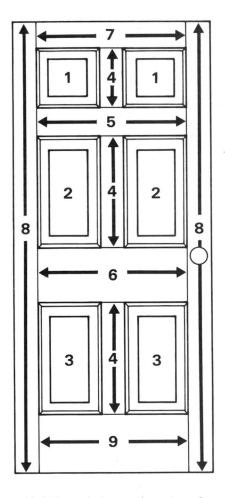

*Illustration 10-3: To get the best results, paint a door with panels in this sequence, starting with the top panels.*

cloth can be placed over the tape to protect more of the floor.

Paint the baseboard with a simple side-to-side brush stroke. Let latex paint dry for 10 to 15 minutes and oil paint for an hour; then pull off the tape at a 45-degree angle. Remove oil paint spots from the floor with hand cleaner; use warm water for latex paint. To coax paint off, fold paper towels over the blade of a flat-head screwdriver or putty knife and rub gently.

If the floor is carpeted, lay a doubled-up drop cloth along the baseboard. Place the paint bucket on the cloth. To keep the brush from touching the carpet, place a 2-foot-long paint guard between it and the baseboard. Paint guards of several lengths are available at paint and hardware stores. Push the guard's metal blade into the crevice between carpet and baseboard, then tilt it away from the wall to force the carpet from the baseboard. This enables you to apply paint below the carpet line. Use a 2½-inch brush for better control, and paint the baseboard with a side-to-side brush stroke, starting from the bottom. Tilt the guard back toward the wall, and gingerly slide it away from the baseboard.

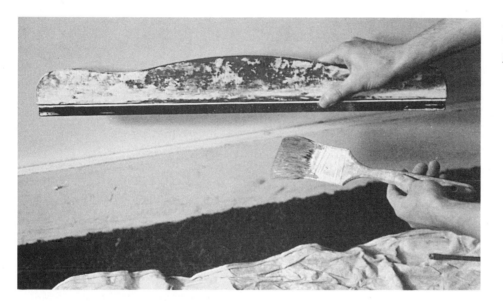

*Photo 10-16: Protect wall-to-wall carpet from paint with a paint guard.*

*Photo 10-17: Apply paint below the carpet line with a 2½-inch brush.*

The carpet will return to its original position, and the paint line will now be covered.

Clean the guard's blade with a paper towel after every insertion so that it doesn't get paint on the carpet hairs. Have a plastic bucket nearby to hold used paper towels.

Each time you insert the guard, overlap the just-painted baseboard about an inch; this keeps you from trying to paint too close to the edge of the metal blade. Refer to Chapter 8 for help in getting paint off carpeting. If only a few carpet hairs are involved, simply let the paint dry and snip them off with scissors.

## Railings

Wooden railings are pretty straightforward. Simply use the trim board technique of first applying the paint across the grain and then smoothing the paint with the grain. Be systematic (paint the underside, sides, and top of one board before moving on to the next), or you're apt to miss whole sides.

Iron railings are the last items of a home's exterior to be painted. Painting with a brush takes a lot of time, so do the job with spray cans. Just before painting, check the railing for rust. Even if you removed all the rust yesterday with a wire brush, the iron probably oxidized overnight and again needs to be wire brushed. Paint iron railings immediately after prepping them.

Apply masking tape where the iron meets floors, steps, or walls, and lay drop cloths to catch the overspray. You can also tape down newspaper for protection, sparing your drop cloths from the paint. Spray the railing using any sequence you wish. Apply enough paint that you won't have to bother spraying a second coat. Remove drops and masking tape, and check for missed areas and drips.

## Gutters and Downspouts

Gutters should be painted the color of the trim paint; downspouts should be painted the color of the trim board or siding directly behind it. That's because these are utility items, not ornamental details, and you want to play them down.

Paint gutters and downspouts while you are doing the trim or siding, rather than save them for later. Regular house paint should adhere perfectly well to the metal.

If you have wooden gutters, coat the inside with roofing tar. Try to do so before painting the trim, so that you can cover any tar spills with trim paint.

## Steps

There's no special trick to painting steps and stairs. Simply paint top to bottom, and move from railings, to posts, to steps in that order. Use a 4-inch brush and plenty of floor enamel paint that is specifically formulated for heavy wear. You may want to mix granulated sand (available at the paint store) into your paint for extra traction on outdoor steps.

Some painters advocate painting every other step at first, so that the stairs can be used while the paint is drying. The remaining steps are then done. I do not recommend this. A drying step may be easily mistaken for a dried one, and the result is paint on shoes, paint on carpeting, and more work. I say paint the whole thing, let it dry, and be done with it.

# INDEX

Note: page numbers in *italic* refer to tables; page numbers in **boldface** refer to photographs and illustrations.